# Funké Koleosho's
# Contemporary
# Nigerian Cuisine

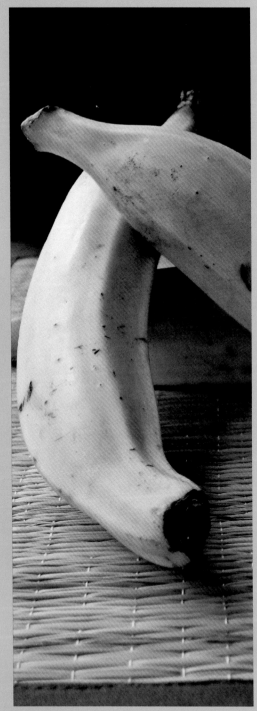

First published in Great Britain, 2009 by

JOK Publishing, United Kingdom

Printed and bound in the United Kingdom by Pitney Bowes UK Ltd.


Content & recipes: Funke Koleosho

Front & back cover design: Kolex Creative Design Services

Food presentation & design: Funke Koleosho

Food nutrition Adviser: Bunmi Dakat

Editing: Olakunle Awosusi

Food Photography: Gavin Bond (TNG Food Photography Ltd.)

Front Cover Photography: Tony Hussey (THP Photo Imaging)


Contemporary Nigerian Cuisine
Copyright: © Funke Koleosho 2009

## ISBN: 9780956148803

**All effort has been made to ensure that the information contained in this book is accurate. The recipes and proportions of ingredients used have been tested but must only be used as a guide. Adjustments and varieties can be made to adapt the recipes to your exact taste and preference.**

# Contents

*Five reasons why you must cook your food yourself:*

*•You will be certain of the ingredients that go into it*
*•You will be guaranteed of a healthy and balanced diet*
*•You will be able to manage your food and dinning budget better and save*
*•You will be able to propagate age old traditions of cooking and passing on 'secret' recipes*
*•You will be educating yourself and others*

*Anon.*

# Foreword

Welcome.

The Contemporary Nigerian Cuisine cookbook brings to you simple and delicious recipes from Nigeria. The recipes have been designed to create nutritionally balanced and well presented dishes that represent some of the most popular delicacies from Nigeria, West Africa.

Authentic spices, condiments and ingredients have been used to create dishes which offer exotic aromas, tastes and flavours.

Easy-to-follow methods have been used to encourage you to try out the recipes and enjoy the delicious resulting dishes with the hope that your perceptions of West African and indeed Nigerian cuisine will change forever.

I invite you to embark on this exciting culinary adventure of discovery.

Funke Koleosho.

Exotic Spices

Exotic Tastes
& Flavours

# Introduction

West African and indeed Nigerian cuisine remains universally untapped and undiscovered. That said, intercontinental exchanges and migration of peoples across the world have caused a growing interest in international cuisines generally. There is an increasing number of people keen to explore tribes and traditions and of course culinary. As a result, some dishes of West African origins such as *egusi*, *jollof* rice, groundnut soup, fried plantains and the barbeque beef known as *suya* have been discovered and are gaining popularity in Europe, Asia and North and South America. The more people try out these dishes the more they find out there is much to discover.

West African cuisine, including Nigerian food, remains the most authentic and unadulterated in the African continent. In comparison, Northern African cuisine has Middle Eastern influences, so are foods from Eastern Africa with Indian (Asian) and Southern Africa, European influences.

African history on the other hand, points out that West African cooking has created or influenced culinary in other parts of the world. Cuisines from the West Indian islands and North and South America show similarities to West African cooking particularly those referred to today as Creole, Soul and Cajun.

The high levels of importation and exportation of local Nigerian food ingredients across continents is an indication that Nigerian food is gaining popularity around the world. This may be due, in part, to the increasing number of Nigerians living in Diaspora and an equally increasing number of foreign nationals taking up employment in Nigeria in light of the oil boom leading to intercultural exchanges. Culinary discovery of tastes and flavours is being made by many from Asia, Europe and the Americas who live and work in Nigeria.

## Perceptions

Internationally, the perception of Nigerian foods, can't lend justice to their actual tastes and goodness. Unless these marvelous and equally nutritious dishes have been sampled, their true place in comparison with cooking from around the world will not be rightfully established.

The most distinguishing factor of Nigerian cuisine is the carbohydrate rich ingredients used to prepare a main dish, served with a sauce, soup or stew containing a combination of fish, meat and an abundance of vegetables. While some may have concerns for diets with high levels of carbohydrates, it must be emphasized that carbohydrates are an essential part of a balanced diet and eating them cannot be ruled out. With the in-depth understanding of the

chemical components of the ingredients and the application of modern techniques to prepare them, moderate amounts of key ingredients can be used to provide nutritionally balanced dishes.

In traditional settings, meals are made using fresh ingredients gathered directly from the farm. These ingredients are organically cultivated, and full of nutrients and goodness. Traditional methods used to prepare the ingredients enhance tastes and flavours as well as preserve wholesomeness.

## Methods

Nigeria is a multicultural nation. It is therefore not surprising that there are different culinary experiences as we move from one region to the other. Cooking styles are dictated by culture and available local farm produce, fruits & vegetables, exotic meats and fish which differ significantly from one geographical area to another.

Traditional methods involve cooking in an open space, over firewood stoves. It is believed that this contributes to flavour development. As more Nigerians emigrate to different parts of the world, foreign methods of cooking are being applied to preparing and cooking traditional Nigerian dishes. For instance, some traditional cooking techniques require extensive preparation and processing, but the application of technology and use of modern equipments greatly reduces time and effort required. These new methods and innovations are welcomed by many, particularly those who live urban lifestyles. Over the years, Nigerian cuisine has evolved through experimentation and modification of methods and ingredients. The growing awareness for healthy eating is also causing people to adjust ingredients and methods to make healthier versions of their favourite dishes.

In view of this, quicker and simpler methods have emerged, opening new lines of enterprise for many. The result is the re-creation of popular Nigerian dishes that still retain their authenticity, but presented in a manner which makes them more appealing to Nigerians and non-Nigerians alike.

## Serving & Presentation

Traditional Nigerian meals are served in dishes made from calabashes, clay or wood. These are deep serving dishes which are ideal for holding both soup and the accompaniments, even though it is also common to have them served up in two separate dishes. Meal times are times for sharing often with family members eating from the same dish! In this cookbook, the author has served and presented dishes in a manner which ensures a nutritional balance and creates a great visual appeal.

Overall the author aims to draw attention to Nigerian foods, and the new methods of preparing and presenting them. It is hoped this will change perceptions and encourage keen cooks to embark on a journey to discover new textures, tastes and flavours.

# Cooking Guide

## Using this cookbook

Efforts have been made to ensure that the recipes in this book are simple and easy to follow in no more than 4 steps. It is advised that you read through the list of ingredients and methods before commencing preparation and cooking. Some recipes may require pre-processing such as marinating or tenderizing, which must be carried out before commencing main preparations and cooking.

Authentic ingredients have been used throughout, some of which are optional and should not significantly affect the final dish if not used. Substitute ingredients or method variations are suggested against each recipe especially for vegetarians. Colourful pictures of resulting dishes are displayed aside the recipes for guidance. Traditional names of the dishes and ingredients have been used with suitable interpretations where possible.

## Finding Ingredients

Ensure that all ingredients required for a recipe are available before cooking begins. Ingredients used for the recipes can be found in Afro-Caribbean food stores and open markets in major cities across the world. Ingredient alternatives may be used but results could differ from the outcomes shown in this cookbook. Many ingredients are now branded, so choice will depend on personal preference. When buying ingredients, seek advice from shop assistants (see page 107).

## Timing

The times indicated for preparing and cooking the ingredients are an approximate guide only. Times may differ depending on techniques applied or utensils and appliances used. Preparation time for each recipe does not include time for marinating or other long hour or overnight pre-processing. Total time is based on the assumption that some cooking or preparation processes are carried out simultaneously.

## Measuring

Both metric and imperial measurements can be used but it is advised to follow the same units of measurement through each recipe. Spoon measurements are level, based on assumptions that teaspoons are 5ml, tablespoons are 10ml and serving spoons are 25ml. A cup is equivalent to 250ml.

## Using oils

Blended olive oil is used in most of the recipes in this book but any vegetable oil of choice can be used. Be aware that extra virgin olive oil is not a suitable cooking oil, but best used as a dressing for salads etc. Blended olive oil is more suitable for cooking. Palm oil and groundnut oil are used to define taste and appearance of some traditional dishes. Vary amount of oil used as preferred.

## Symbols Used

Shadowed boxes contain nutritional facts.

Double line boxes contain author's notes for cooks on variations and/or suggestions for optimal results.

Shaded boxes contain researched information & facts.

Recipes with this symbol are suitable for, or may be modified to suit, vegetarians.

Indicates recipes which contain chillis. Use of chilli is optional but taste and flavour development may be affected.

## Base sauce

As you will discover, majority of Nigerian dishes are created by making a base sauce generally referred to as "*ata obe, ofe or miya*". The main components are fresh tomatoes, chilli, onions and sweet peppers.

Proportions of individual ingredient used depend on personal preferences. A pot of stew can be prepared in advance and used to create other dishes.

## Using chilli

Nigerians eat a lot of chillis in comparison with other African nations. There is even a popular adage which says "a life without chilli is a weak life!". Chillis are used a great deal in traditional cooking. Most of the recipes in this cookbook require the use of chilli but their use is optional. There are numerous varieties of chillis and research has proven their nutritional benefits as being rich in minerals and vitamins A & C.

Chillis are also believed to act as an effective decongestant, blood thinning agent and an aid to digestion. They provide a unique flavour and aroma which define the taste of the final dish.

The scotch bonnet chilli, (*ata-rodo*), is the most widely used in Nigerian cooking and is rated as Hot-Extra-Hot. Care should be taken when handling them. Removing their seeds before using, can reduce heat. Finely chopping and frying before adding to your cooking, instead of blending with other ingredients, may also reduce degree of heat. Caution: using and eating chillis must be avoided by those who cannot tolerate hot spicy foods.

## Using seasoning cubes

Seasoning cubes are used as a substitute for stock. There are different brands and flavours including fish, vegetables, chicken or beef. Local ingredients are also being used to create seasoning cubes such as dried smoked crayfish and locust bean. Locust bean seasoning cubes called *dadawa* is branded by Cadbury Nigeria. They are produced in small cubes, and can readily be found in African food stores.

## Vegetarian cooking

There are a variety of dishes suitable for vegetarians even though the practice of vegetarianism is not widespread in Nigeria.
The abundance of root and leafy vegetables which form the staple diet of Nigerians can be used in a variety of mouth watering and nutritious meals to suit vegetarians. Exotic fruits, seeds and nuts are also available to use in stews, soups and sauces which are great for vegetarians. Most recipes in this cookbook can be modified to suit vegetarians.

# Condiments & Spices

Condiments and spices define taste and appearance of Nigerian dishes. Below are some of the key condiments and spices used in the recipes contained in this book, most of which can be found in Afro-Caribbean grocery shops and African food stores/supermarkets or ethnic food markets.

## Cameroun pepper mix (picture G)

A special blend of different aromatic herbs and chillis, the main being sun dried and ground cameroun pepper. Desirable for its unique aroma and heat. Very hot, use sparingly. Similar to 'ata jos'.

## Ground smoked crayfish (picture E)

Made by grinding smoked and dried crayfish (picture I) into powder. Used in vegetable dishes such as ogbonna, okra, 'egusi' and 'efo riro', desired for its flavour and aroma. Also available as a seasoning cube.

## Locust beans (picture F)

Ancient and very traditional condiment used in most parts of Nigeria. Very versatile and used in many dishes. Locally called iru, dadawa or dawadawa. Great tasting with very strong pungent smell which is off putting for some but desirable by many. Defines taste, appearance and flavour of dishes in which it is used. Rich in vitamins A, D & E. Locust beans now available as seasoning cubes called dadawa cubes. Frozen or powdered locust beans can also be found in African food stores and markets.

## Ogbonna (picture C)

Derived from oil seeds of the bush mango. Typically used to thicken soups and widely desired for its taste and aroma. Rich in oil soluble minerals.

## Suya mix (picture D)

A blend of spices (typically cloves, garlic), herbs (dried thyme), roots (ginger), barks (believed to act as an aphrodisiac), chilli powder and groundnut paste (kulilkuli). Seasoning cubes and dadawa powder may also be added. Suya mix is used to make meat or fish barbeques. Branded suya mixes are available to purchase in African food stores. Individual component ingredients are also available for purchase so it is possible (and recommended) to blend your own suya mix using preferred proportions of individual key ingredients. Branded Suya mixes typically have a high chilli content so use with caution.

## Seasoning cubes (picture J)

Seasoning cubes are made from stock (beef, chicken or vegetables) and widely used in Nigerian cooking as a substitute for liquid stock. In recent times, crayfish and dadawa seasoning cubes have been developed to use in place of ground crayfish and fermented locust beans respectively.

Nigerian seasoning cubes are smaller than those found in Europe; one bouillon cube is often equivalent to 3 seasoning cubes. To use, crush, dissolve in hot water or add whole to cooking or sizzling dishes. They generally contain additional spices, salt and flavour enhancers. Please read the label before use. The two most popular brands used in Nigeria are Knorr and Maggi.

## Ground Chilli Powder (picture B)

Excess harvest of chilli peppers are preserved by sun drying and grinding into flakes or powder. Used in place of fresh chillis in cooking and for spicing up dishes or meals. Also used as a table condiment.

## Pepper soup mix (picture H)

A combination of herbs, seeds, pods (picture A) and spices (African nutmeg, aniseeds, alligator pepper, ground ginger and ground chilli) which creates one of Nigeria's most enjoyed dishes. Branded pepper soup mixes are readily available but their components vary. Typically high in chilli so use with caution. Best to source individual ingredients to create own pepper soup mix, to achieve preferred taste and flavour. Dominant ingredients are achi, utazi, 'scent leaves', (efirin or bush basil), and African nutmeg, (kanafuru or ehuru). Originally believed to have medicinal properties, any herb of preference may be added.

# Glossary of traditional ingredients:

Here are descriptions of traditional ingredients used in the recipes contained in this cookbook. Most of them can be found in African food stores and large supermarkets or open markets in large cities across the world.

◀ **Pumpkin Leaves**
Found mostly in the eastern parts of Nigeria. Locally called *ugwu* and used in a variety of dishes. Offers same nutritional values as most dark green leafy vegetable. Used in dishes such as *edikang-ikong*, *egusi* soup. (pg 53)

**Bitter Leaves**
Called *ewuro* by the *Yorubas*. Bitter leaves have a distinct bitter taste and believed to have medicinal properties. Prepared by thinly slicing and rubbing with salt to reduce bitterness. Cooked with ground melon/pumpkin seeds in soups.

▼ **Garden eggs**
Different varieties but are typically white or green. Belong to same family as aubergines. Eaten raw or stewed (pg 71). Traditionally served to welcome visitors in *Igbo* land.

▲ **Cassava granules**
Fermented & toasted cassava granules (*gari*). Eaten as a snack by soaking in ice cold water with sugar and groundnuts. Also made into *eba*.

▲ **Yam flour**
Sun dried yam slices, milled into flour called *elubo*. Plantains and cassava are also processed in this way.

**Pounded yam flour** ▶
A product of recent application of modern techniques, pounded yam flour was developed to simplify the task of pounding yam with mortar and pestle. Increasingly used by urban dwellers to make pounded yam (pg 67).

Yams are the main staple source of carbohydrate in Nigeria and they come in different varieties, which dictates their use. Eaten pounded, roasted, boiled or chipped and served with vegetables. Yams are rich in vitamin C, minerals and high in fibre.

The different varieties have a different appearance by which they are identified. The featured variety is called '*puna*'

## Uses:

Yams can be boiled, roasted/baked or fried, like their European equivalent - potatoes. They are also dried and powdered into yam flour. The variety of the yam determines how best it may be cooked or processed. *Native name(s) isu, doya.*

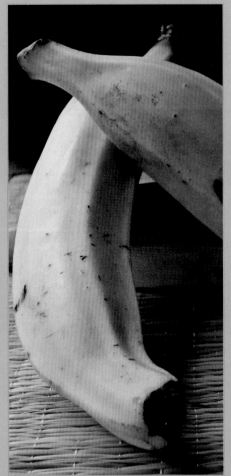

## ▲ Brown beans

Affordable source of protein. Widely eaten as an accompaniment to other dishes. Cooked in a variety of ways including peeling, blending and steaming to make *moin moin* or *ekuru* and frying to make a*kara* (pg 81, 93,96). Can also be cooked in a mash with rice or sweet corn. Two main varieties; *oloyin* (with naturally sweet taste) and *olo1&2.*

## ◀ Plantains

Plantains belong to the same family as bananas. They are eaten and loved for their sugary taste especially when fully ripe. Can be cooked in their different stages of ripeness. A good source of minerals and slow release energy.

## Uses:

**Fried** as '*dodo*', '*crisps*' or '*kelewele*', **roasted** as '*boli*', **dried** and powdered into '*elubo-ogede*' to make *amala*, **boiled**, or cooked with other vegetables such as beans. Stage of ripeness dictates best cooking method and resulting dish.

## Okra

Often referred to as ladies finger or '*gumbo*'.

A good source of many nutrients including vitamins B6 & C, calcium and folic acid. The smaller, younger okra fingers are better in terms of minerals and nutrients. The larger ones are more woody and tough to eat. Click the tip of an okra finger off to check tenderness.

Okra is desired for its texture and taste. It becomes gelatinous when boiled, a desirable property for some. Slightly fry or sauté okra to reduce or remove slime before adding to soups or stews.

## Pumpkin / Melon Seeds

Pumpkin seeds are an excellent source of minerals, such as zinc, magnesium & manganese. Also contain B vitamins & vitamin K.

Pumpkin seeds are rich in good fats, and are a good source of omega 3 & 6, essential fats needed for hormone balance, brain function and skin health. The seeds are ground and cooked with spinach, bitter leaves or *ugwu*. They are also ground and fried into snacks called *robo*.

## Sugar Cane

Can be eaten raw. Its juice is squeezed and used as a sweetener. Full of minerals and vitamins. (pg 103)

## Jute leaves

Dark green vegetables rich in minerals and vitamins. Prepared by removing leaves from the stalk, wash and blend finely with a little amount of water.
This blend is boiled adding condiments like locust beans, ground crayfish or seasoning cubes, as preferred. Referred to as *ewedu*, and best eaten in combination with bean soup (*gbegiri*) served with yam flour (*amala*).

## Spinach / Greens

Spinach and greens are eaten regularly cooked in stews or soups. Preparing them require meticulous picking of tender leaves and stalk.

Larger leaves and stalks are preferred as they are most ideal for steaming or simmering. Leaves can be softened by blanching in hot water or in the microwave before adding to stews or soups.

14

Palm oil is the staple cooking oil used all over Nigeria and is desirable for its rich vibrant reddish-orange colour. Made from palm kernels, palm oil contains some saturated fats but also has a high ratio of "good fats" similar to those found in olive oil. Palm oil is increasingly being used in commercial food production as a healthy alternative to hydrogenated fats.

Palm Oil ▶

Palm oil is rich in beta-carotenes which support the production of vitamin A. It is also high in vitamin E, a natural anti-oxidant. From all indications, pure, unadulterated palm oil is ideal and safe to eat when used moderately. It is also believed to have medicinal properties and useful for treating ingestion of poison or soothing burns and skin irritations.

## Smoked Fish/Dried Fish / Stockfish

These are made by smoking or drying fish such as cod, hake, mackerel and catfish. They contribute flavour and texture to dishes as well as provide nutritional benefits such as protein, B vitamins, omega oil and minerals. In nutritional value, for instance, 1 stockfish is the equivalent of 4 fresh cod!

To use dried fish, they are first prepared by soaking in hot salted water. Thorough washing is also necessary. Preparing stockfish requires boiling to tenderize and soften it. Dried fish may be used in place of, or in addition to meat or fresh fish in some dishes. Stockfish is locally known as *panla* or *okporoko*.

## Garlic

Garlic (*ayu*) is generally believed to have medicinal values. Used in marinades & sauces. Considered to help lower cholesterol.

## Red sweet peppers ▶

Provides the red vibrant colour of Nigerian soups sauces and other dishes. Also contributes to the consistency of sauces and stews. The more peppers used the thicker the sauce made. Also called *tatase*, red peppers are not hot, but high in vitamins A & C and used in everyday cooking. The varieties found in Nigeria are smaller than those found in Europe.

## ▼ Scotch Bonnet

Used to give spice and heat to dishes. Has a pungent aroma which can be perceive during cooking. There are two main varieties, red and yellow. The yellow variety is thought to have slightly less heat and more of the pungent aroma which some prefer over the red variety. Chillis generally are nutritionally rich in minerals and vitamins A & C.

They are believed to have medicinal properties. Medical research shows they act as an effective decongestant, thin the blood and aid digestion. They should be used with caution. Removing the seeds before using is believed to reduce the strength of the heat.

## Red onions ▶

Red onions, (more purple in appearance), are the variety found in Nigeria. Eaten raw, used as garnish or cooked in stews, soups and other dishes. Also used to season meats.

15

# CHAPTER 1

# MEAT & POULTRY

*Beef*

A variety of meat and poultry ranging from goat, lamb, beef, chicken, duck, guinea fowl and turkey are used in Nigerian cooking. There is also some, although limited, use of pork in Nigerian cooking. Some traditional dishes are made with game particularly 'grass-cutter' (*oya*) and deer (*etu*); which are popular local delicacies. It is common for stews and soups to contain different types of meat all allowed to cook and sizzle together impacting different textures and flavours.

Nigerians favour different parts of a livestock such as the oxtail, cow-foot, hide and organ meats. These are enjoyed for their varying textures and flavours which are further developed through processes such as boiling, frying, grilling, sun drying and even smoking. Meat and poultry accompany main dishes and may also be used to make snacks.

# BEEF IN SPICY PEPPER SAUCE

*Preparation Time:* 10 minutes
*Marinating time:* 30 minutes
*Cooking Time:* 45 minutes
*Serves:* 4-6 people

The spicy pepper sauce is versatile and used daily in a variety of ways. Traditionally made by cooking blended tomatoes, red peppers and onions in earthenware pots in a slow cooking process, the result is a rich and thick sauce eaten with almost anything.

*Native name(s): obe, ofe, miya*

*700g beef, cut into bite size pieces •*
*½ medium size red sweet pepper, remove seeds •*
*1 medium size onion, skin & cut into quarters •*
*1 small (yellow) scotch bonnet, remove seeds (optional) •*
*6-8 medium fresh tomatoes or 2 tins of peeled plum tomatoes •*
*150ml cooking oil •*
*1 clove of garlic, crush •*
*2 seasoning cubes •*
*½ teaspoon curry power •*
*2 sprigs of fresh thyme •*
*Spring onion, slice •*

**1** Place beef pieces in a bowl. Add 1 seasoning cube, some salt, thyme, curry powder and garlic. Work spices into beef pieces and let marinate for at least 30 minutes. Add 2 cups of water and boil for about 15 minutes. Turn heat off and allow to cool. Remove boiled meat pieces and briskly fry in hot oil or alternatively, grill for about 10 minutes. Sieve and save stock for use in step 2.

**2** Blend tomatoes, peppers, onion and scotch bonnet, (if using), until smooth. Heat oil in a pot and add the blended mix. Add stock and stir, then add up to 750ml of hot water. Allow to boil for about 10 minutes under high heat then turn heat down, and simmer for another 10-15 minutes.

**3** Add meat pieces to the cooking sauce. Add second seasoning cube. Stir well and continue to cook for another 5 minutes or until meat is tender as preferred. Add 1 cup of hot water to adjust consistency as preferred, stir well. Add salt to taste.

**4** Garnish with spring onions and serve with boiled rice or pasta. Can also be served with other dishes such as pounded yam and vegetables.

Olive oil is increasingly being used in Nigerian cooking as a healthier alternative to oils with high levels of bad fat. It is important to note that **Extra Virgin** olive oil is not ideal for heating or cooking. Use blended olive oil instead.

### Cook's note
For the best results, choose ripe and sweet (plum) tomatoes to avoid the sharp/acidic taste associated with unripe tomatoes.
**Scotch bonnet** defines heat and can be increased or decreased as preferred. **Avoid** its use completely to make dish less spicy. Adding whole chilli (rather than blending it) to the cooking sauce will impart flavour and taste but less heat. Using palm oil for this recipe will create a more authentic taste.

# SUYA

*Preparation Time:* 10 minutes
*Marinating time:* 120 minutes
*Cooking Time:* 20 minutes
*Serves:* 4 people

### Cook's note

**Caution:** *Suya* mixes contain varying amounts of chilli. Some may also contain nuts. Check package carefully. This recipe can be created without using groundnut paste, but taste and flavour may not develop fully.

*Suya* is skewered meat cooked over hot smoky barbeque fires. It originates from the northern part of Nigeria where there is an abundance of meat, but eaten all over the country particularly in urban towns and cities where it is used as part of social entertainment.

A blend of spices gives *suya* its unique taste that makes it so popular. Ingredients include ground peanuts, dried locust beans, powdered herbs, roots, seasoning and salt. Pre-packed *suya* spices are readily available in African food stores. *Suya* can be made using a variety of meat or fish.

*500g of beef with some streak of fat •*
*100ml groundnut oil (or any vegetable oil) •*
*1 small red onion, thinly slice •*
*3 tablespoons of suya mix (use more or less depending on chilli content) •*
*4 medium salad tomatoes, wash and slice •*
*Lettuce, slice •*
*2 tablespoons of groundnut paste (or crunchy peanut butter) •*
*2 seasoning cubes •*
*Small piece of ginger, grate •*

**1** Thinly slice beef into sheet-like pieces. Rinse and place pieces in a large mixing bowl. Add the *suya* mix and crumbled seasoning cubes. Add the groundnut oil, grated ginger and groundnut paste. Work spices into the meat and allow to marinate for at least 2 hours.

**2** Skewer the beef pieces as you desire. Heat up an iron griddle (you may also use an open barbeque grill), and place the skewered beef. Allow to cook for about 3-5 minutes on each side or until meat is cooked to your preference. Avoid burning by regularly turning skewered beef.
**OR**
Alternatively, place beef pieces in an oven dish and cook in a heated oven (190 gas mark 5) for about 15-20 minutes, turning meat pieces occasionally.

**3** Serve *suya* with sliced lettuce, onions and tomatoes and a chilled drink.

If using other types of meat, amount of spices required and time for cooking may vary slightly. There are different brands of *suya* mix on the market, and they vary in content which may give varying results. Best option is to personally blend *suya* spices as preferred using the different component spices.

Some traditional barks and spices used to season *suya* are believed to have aphrodisiac properties.

# OXTAIL PEPPER SOUP

*Preparation Time:* 10 minutes
*Cooking Time:* 50 minutes
*Serves:* 4 people

Pepper soup pods & seeds are believed to have properties which help relief stress and aid absorption of nutrients.

Soups are eaten on different occasions and due to their high content of herbs, barks and spices they are thought to have medicinal properties. People suffering from or recovering from an illness will normally be served soup.

Simple and light soups are eaten as social meals in bars (*pepper soup joints*) or restaurants. Bolder soups are eaten as a complete meal usually with added carbohydrate accompaniments such as potatoes, yams, *eko* or hard dough bread.

400g oxtail •
1 tablespoon groundnut paste or crunchy peanut butter (optional) •
½ teaspoon cameroun pepper (very hot but aromatic, optional) •
2 tablespoons pepper soup mix (more or less depending on brand and chilli content) •
A handful of pepper soup making pods and seeds (see picture above) •
50ml cooking oil •
2 medium tomatoes •
¼ red sweet pepper •
A handful of freshly chopped basil •
2 seasoning cubes •
2 sprigs fresh thyme •
1 teaspoon curry powder •
2 medium slices of yam (or 2 small potatoes), cut into chunks •
1 sprig of spring onion, finely slice •

**1** Season oxtail pieces with thyme, curry and seasoning cubes. Add enough water to boil for about 25 minutes or until just tender and meat fall off the bone, (use a pressure cooker to cook oxtail faster). Remove bones and separate meat pieces. Sieve and retain stock for use in step 3.

**2** Blend tomatoes and pepper with 1 cup of water. Pour into a large pot, add 1 litre of water, then add the pepper soup mix, cameroun pepper (if using) and the pepper soup pods/seeds. Add oil and boil for 15 minutes to allow spices to infuse. Allow to stand for about 10 minutes. Then sieve the sediments (the spent pods/spices).

**3** Return the emerging soup to the stove and add meat pieces, also add the retained stock, stir slowly under low heat. Add the groundnut paste (if using), stir well. Allow to simmer for about 5 minutes. Add the yam chunks, simmer for 10 minutes. Add a cup of hot water if required to adjust consistency. Allow to cook until yam becomes soft. Add a handful of basil, stir and taste for salt.

**4** Garnish with sliced spring onions and serve immediately with hard dough bread.

### Cook's note
Any type of meat can be used for this recipe such as goat meat. Contents of pepper soup mix differ with brand. Use of cameroun pepper is optional.

# ASSORTED MEAT STEW

*Preparation Time:* 10 minutes
*Marinating time:* 30 minutes
*Cooking Time:* 40 minutes
*Serves:* 4-6 people

*300g beef, trim & cut into bite size pieces, wash •*
*200g cow foot, wash, salt & cook until very tender. Remove bone and cut into small bite size pieces •*
*200g honeycomb tripe, cut into small bite size pieces, wash, salt & cook until tender. •*
*½ medium size red sweet pepper, remove stalk & seeds. Cut into quarters, wash •*
*1 small (yellow) scotch bonnet, remove seeds (optional) •*
*6-8 medium fresh tomatoes (or 2 tins of peeled plum tomatoes) •*
*1 medium size onion. Skin & cut into quarters •*
*150ml of cooking or blended olive oil •*
*1 sprig fresh thyme •*
*1 teaspoon curry powder •*
*1 clove of garlic, crush •*
*1 stalk of spring onions, chop •*
*3 seasoning cubes •*

It is very common in Nigerian cooking to use different types of meat in one stew. Their different textures and flavours contribute to the overall taste and enjoyment of this recipe.

**1** Place beef pieces in a bowl. Add some salt, thyme, one seasoning cube, curry powder and garlic. Work spices into meat and let marinate for at least 30 minutes. Then add 500ml of water and boil until just tender. Cool, remove meat pieces, sieve and retain stock for use in step 2.

**2** Place the tomatoes, peppers, onion and scotch bonnet (if using), in the blender and blend till smooth. Heat oil in a sauce pan and add the blend. Add the stock, stir. Add 750ml of water. Allow to cook for 10 minutes under high heat then turn heat down and simmer for 20 minutes.

**3** In the meantime, briskly fry meat and tripe pieces for about 5 minutes. Drain excess oil. Add the fried meat and tripe pieces to the simmering sauce and stir. Also add the cow foot pieces. Stir gently, then add remaining 2 seasoning cubes, allow to simmer for a further 10 minutes or until meat is tender. Taste for salt.

**4** Garnish with spring onions and serve with boiled rice, pasta or hard dough bread. Also served with vegetable soups and pounded yam.

*Using fresh thyme imparts more aroma and flavour to this dish.*

### Cook's note
Other meat types can be used for this dish, such as chicken, duck, fried fish etc. Cow foot is tough and requires long cooking. Boiling can be simplified by using a pressure cooker. When well cooked, cow foot has a very soft and jelly-like texture. Hot recipe but use of chilli is optional.

# SPAGHETTI

*Preparation Time:* 10 minutes
*Marinating time:* 15 minutes
*Cooking Time:* 30 minutes
*Serves:* 4 people

Spaghetti has become quite popular as an alternative to rice. Cooked broken into pieces rather than in its long stringy form as it is eaten in Europe.

*400g beef. Trim & cut into thin stripes, wash •*
*½ medium size red sweet pepper, remove stalk & seeds, wash •*
*1 small scotch bonnet, remove seeds (optional) •*
*4 medium fresh tomatoes (or 1 tin of peeled plum tomatoes) •*
*½ medium size onion. Skin & cut into quarters •*
*Blended olive oil •*
*2 seasoning cubes •*
*2 cups of water •*
*1 teaspoon curry powder •*
*300g spaghetti •*
*1 sprig fresh thyme •*
*1 clove of garlic, finely chop •*
*Handful of green peas •*

**1** Place beef pieces in a bowl. Add some salt, thyme, curry powder and garlic. Work spices into meat and let marinate for a few minutes.

**2** Place the tomatoes, peppers, onion and scotch bonnet (if using), in the blender and blend till smooth. Heat 75ml of oil in a sauce pan and add the blended mix. Add 2 cups of water and stir. Allow to cook for 10 minutes under high heat then turn heat down, and continue to simmer for a further 15 minutes.

**3** Meanwhile, heat 100ml of oil in a separate sauce pan, add the marinated beef and 1 seasoning cube. Stir until browned. Add the simmering sauce and stir well. Continue to cook until meat is tender. Simultaneously, break-up the spaghetti and cook in salted boiling water until soft. Drain excess water off from the spaghetti and stir into the sauce. Add peas and stir again. Simmer for about 2 minutes.

**4** Serve hot.

**Cook's note**
The amount of spaghetti stirred into the sauce will depend on preference. Stirring a little at a time will ensure that the right proportions are reached. Use of chilli is optional.

*Meat & Poultry*

Vegetarian option: meat substitutes can be used instead of beef.

# SPICY FRIED CHICKEN

*Preparation Time:* 10 minutes
*Marinating time:* 60 minutes
*Cooking Time:* 10 minutes
*Serves:* 4 people

Chicken is eaten widely and regularly therefore spices are used to create a different taste every time. Local fowls or laying chickens are preferred by Nigerians due to their slightly tougher texture which is desirable to endure the long cooking process they are put through; typically boiling, frying and stewing.

*8 chicken thighs, skin and wash. Remove bone and cut into bite size pieces •*
*100ml blended olive oil or vegetable oil •*
*1 clove of garlic •*
*½ green pepper •*
*2 seasoning cubes •*
*2 sprigs of fresh thyme •*
*1 teaspoon curry powder •*
*½ teaspoon cameroun pepper (very hot, optional) •*
*Handful of diced green and yellow peppers •*
*2 tablespoons breadcrumbs •*
*1 inch of ginger •*
*½ teaspoon of ground or freshly milled nutmeg •*

**1** Place chicken pieces in a bowl, add thyme. Using a small mortar and pestle, pound the green pepper, ginger and garlic. Add to chicken. Also add nutmeg, crushed seasoning cube, curry powder and salt. Add the oil and mix well to distribute spices into chicken pieces. Sprinkle cameroun pepper (if using). Lastly add the breadcrumbs a little a time. Avoid adding too much. Give it a final mix and allow to marinate for at least 1 hour.

**2** Under moderately high heat, deep fry chicken pieces for about 4-5 minutes, or until outer parts of chicken become crispy as desired. Drain excess oil.

**3** Garnish with briskly fried fresh diced green and yellow peppers. Serve.

### Cook's note
Chicken wings or breast may be used for this recipe but cooking time will differ. Use of cameroon pepper is optional.

The skin contains most of the fat in a chicken. Remove skin before cooking. Separately grill chicken skin until crispy to remove all fat.

# FRIED PLANTAIN

Locally called *dodo* and usually served as a starter, snack or as an accompaniment to rice or bean dishes.

- *2 chicken breasts, cut into small pieces*
- *2 (just) ripe plantains, peel & dice*
- *1 seasoning cube*
- *¼ green pepper, dice*
- *¼ yellow pepper, dice*
- *¼ red pepper, dice*
- *Pinch of freshly chopped thyme*
- *¼ red onion, dice*

**1** Rinse and place chicken pieces in a large mixing bowl. Add the thyme and crumbled seasoning cube. Add salt. Work spices into the chicken. Deep fry until golden brown. Drain excess oil and set aside.

**2** Deep fry the plantain piece, drain and set aside. Briskly fry peppers and onion pieces, drain.

**3** In a colander, place the fried plantain, chicken, peppers and onion. Add some seasoning salt (if you wish) and toss to evenly distribute. Serve.

*Preparation Time*: 10 minutes
*Cooking Time*: 30 minutes
*Serves*: 2 people

# STICK MEAT

A delicious snack or starter. Can be served with rice dishes. Typically made with chicken or turkey gizzards, any type of meat can be used for this recipe.

250g of turkey breast (or beef), wash & cut into bite size pieces •
1 clove of garlic •
10 small cherry tomatoes, wash •
1 seasoning cube •
1 green pepper •
1 red pepper •
fresh thyme •
1 small red onion •

**1** Place turkey pieces in a large mixing bowl. Add some thyme and crumbled seasoning cube. Crush and add garlic and salt. Work spices into the meat. Marinate for 1 hour. Boil for 3-6 minutes. Leave turkey pieces in juice for another hour or two. Drain and deep fry for about 3 minutes or until golden brown and well cooked. Place on kitchen towel to remove excess oil.

**2** Cut onion & peppers to large square pieces in proportion with fried turkey pieces.

**3** Skewer turkey pieces, peppers, onions & tomatoes alternately. Brush on some oil & grill lightly and serve.

*Preparation Time:* 10 minute
*Marinating Time:* 60 minutes
*Cooking Time:* 30 minutes
*Serves:* 4 people

CHAPTER 2

# FISH & SEAFOOD

*Smoked prawns*

Fish is a healthy alternative to meat and is plentiful in Nigeria particularly in the southern regions close to the ocean and areas around the rivers Niger and Benue. There is an overwhelming variety of fresh seafood including the catfish; black and grey varieties, tilapia, snappers, crabs, snails, shrimps & prawns, lobsters, clams, periwinkles and so on. There is also the *eja osan*, a popular delicacy of the *Yorubas*, classified as fish for the elites!

There is also a variety of frozen imported fish used in cooking more affordable and equally healthy meals such as mackerel, hake and ladyfish.

Fish is often eaten whole or as chunky cutlets depending on size. Steaming, stewing, frying and barbequing are common methods of cooking fish. Stewed fresh fish (*obe eja tutu*) is preferably made more spicy. Smoked and dried fish (*okporoko, panla*) are used to create some very authentic dishes due to the aroma and flavours they contribute.

# CATFISH IN SPICY PEPPER SAUCE

*Preparation Time:* 15 minutes
*Cooking Time:* 30 minutes
*Serves:* 4 people

Catfish, is a delicacy that can be eaten fresh or dried. Hot and spicy fish stews are often eaten on cold rainy days.

½ *medium size red sweet pepper, remove stalk & seed, wash* •
*6 catfish cutlets, wash in water with a squeeze of lemon juice* •
*1 small (yellow) scotch bonnet, (optional) remove seeds* •
*6-8 medium fresh tomatoes (or 2 tins of peeled plum tomatoes)* •
*1 medium size onion. Skin & cut into quarters* •
*100ml cooking or blended olive oil* •
*3 seasoning cubes* •
*Fish seasoning* •

**1** Rub fish with some fish seasoning or salt. Set aside.

**2** Blend the pepper, tomatoes, onion and scotch bonnet (if using) into a smooth paste. Heat oil in a sauce pan and add the blend. Add 750ml of water and allow to boil for about 15 minutes under medium heat. Add seasoning cubes and stir.

**3** Turn heat down and add fish, cover sauce pan and simmer for 5-10 minutes for the fish to cook. Taste for salt.

**4** Serve with 'amala' and 'ewedu' (see pg 56). The spicy pepper sauce can also be served with boiled rice.

### Cook's note
Tilapia, salmon, fried hake or snapper can be used instead of catfish. Thickness and sauce consistency can be adjusted to individual preference by adding water and stirring well during the cooking process. . Use of chilli is optional, but adding it sliced rather than blending may reduce heat.

Catfish is a rich source of essential fatty acids; omega 3.

# FISH PEPPER SOUP

*Preparation Time:* 10 minutes
*Cooking Time:* 40 minutes
*Serves:* 3 people

Fish pepper soup is simple and often eaten as a starter. Originating from eastern and river side parts of Nigeria, the fisherman's wife traditionally makes fish soup from leftovers of her husband's catch. These leftovers include small fish, crabs, periwinkles and so on.

Whatever type of fish used, a well prepared fish soup always makes a hearty evening meal that can be served with a variety of accompaniments such as starch, *gari*, yams or '*eko*'.

A handful of pepper soup seeds and pods •
5 dried 'scent leaves' (efirin) or bush basil •
A handful of freshly chopped basil •
2-3 tablespoons pepper soup mix depending on brand and chilli content •
1 tablespoon groundnut paste or peanut butter (this gives soup some texture but use is optional) •
1 large ripe tomato, finely chop •
1 medium fresh bream •
25ml vegetable or olive oil •
3 seasoning cubes •
1 litre water •

**1** Wash fish in water with a squeeze of lemon. Cut into chunks. Drain and rub with some salt then set aside.

**2** In a large pot, fry the chopped tomatoes in oil for about 2 minutes, then add 1 litre of water and bring to the boil. Add the pepper soup mix, pepper soup pods, *scent leaves* and seasoning cubes. Stir and leave to boil (under moderate heat) for 10 minutes to allow spices to infuse. Turn off heat, allow to stand for 5 minutes and sieve off the sediments (the spices).

**3** Return to the stove and continue to cook under low heat. Add the groundnut paste (if using) and stir in. Add fish, cover and simmer for 5 minutes adding some hot water (about 1 cup or as required) to adjust consistency. Add salt to taste. Add a handful of basil. Stir and simmer for 2-5 minutes or until fish is cooked.

**4** Serve hot.

### Cook's note
Any preferred fish can be used in this recipe such as tilapia or catfish. Caution; chilli content of pepper soup mixes varies with brand.
If available, fresh scent leaves should also be used.

Vegetarian option:
substitute fish with wild mushrooms and other vegetables of choice.

This recipe contains nuts. Nut allergy sufferers should avoid the use of groundnut paste or peanut butter. Making this dish without nuts will still create a good result.

Fish & Seafood

# FRIED FISH WITH RICE & BEANS

*Preparation Time:* 25 minutes
*Cooking Time:* 30 minutes
*Serves:* 4 people

Slowly cooked rice and beans served as a nutritionally complete meal. You will enjoy the resulting creamy dish from this recipe. Suitable for vegetarians when served without the fish.

*1 medium red bream, clean and wash in water with 2 tablespoons of lemon, cut into 4 portions •*
*1 cup of African brown beans, pick chaffs and stones. Wash •*
*2 cups of easy cook long grain rice, wash (easy cook basmati can also be used) •*
*50ml cooking or blended olive oil •*
*50ml of palm oil •*
*1 teaspoon chilli powder (optional) •*
*Some thinly sliced green and yellow peppers for garnish •*
*2 medium ripe tomatoes finely chop •*
*1 large onion, finely chop •*
*1-2 litre of water •*
*2 seasoning cubes •*

**1** Rub fish with some salt and allow to stand for about 15 minutes.

**2** In a large enough pot, heat 50ml of oil and add the chopped onions and tomatoes. Add a pinch of salt and allow to brown. Add 1 litre of water then add the beans. Boil for about 10 minutes, then add the chilli powder if using. Cover pot and continue to cook until beans become soft. Alternatively, you can cook beans in a pressure cooker.

**3** Turn heat down check beans for softness. At this point beans should be just soft to the touch. Add 2 cups of hot water, (or enough water to cook rice). Then add the washed rice, seasoning cubes, cover tightly and allow to simmer until rice becomes soft. Add palm oil and stir in until evenly distributed. Simmer for another 5 minutes, add some hot water if required to adjust consistency. Add salt to taste.

**4** Simultaneously deep fry fish, drain excess oil. Garnish with sautéed peppers and serve with the rice and beans.

Vegetarian option:
serve meal without fish.

**Cook's note**
The proportion of beans to rice depends on individual preference. You may use more beans or rice as desired. Use of chilli is optional.

Fish & seafood

# COCONUT RICE & FISH IN COCONUT SAUCE

*Preparation Time:* 10 minutes
*Cooking Time:* 30 minutes
*Serves:* 2 people

It is thought that the *Calabaris* of Nigeria originated the use of coconut milk in cooking, a style that is being adopted across the country. Cooking with coconut milk produces a very rich and creamy dish like the one from this recipe.

*50g of chicken or ox liver, salt and boil. Drain and dice •*
*2 cutlets of fresh catfish (the gray variety, obokun) or any oily fish of choice, wash in water with a splash of lemon juice, allow to stand in salted water for about 15 minutes. •*
*Handful of diced green pepper•*
*4 medium tomatoes •*
*2 sprigs of fresh thyme •*
*½ red pepper •*
*1 onion •*
*1 small yellow scotch bonnet, remove seeds (optional) •*
*1 cup of coconut milk •*
*2 cups of easy cook long grain rice, wash and drain •*
*2 seasoning cubes •*
*500ml of water •*
*50ml cooking or blended olive oil •*

**1** Blend tomatoes, peppers, scotch bonnet (if using) and onions into smooth paste. Heat oil in a pot and add blend. Cook for about 10 minutes under high heat.

**2** Add the coconut milk and bring to the boil. Turn heat down and simmer for about 10 minutes. Add thyme, seasoning cubes, and pinch of salt. Add the fish and allow to cook for about 5 minutes. Dish out fish onto a plate with 2-3 serving spoons of sauce and set aside.

**3** Add rice to the remaining sauce, and also add some hot water enough to cook the rice. Cover and simmer until rice is soft. Add diced liver and green peppers. Stir well.

**4** Serve rice with fish.

**Cook's notes**
Depending on preference, other meats or vegetables pieces can be added to this dish. Easy cook basmati rice can also be used in this recipe. Use of chilli is optional.

Vegetarian option:
recipe can be made without fish and chicken liver pieces.

Coconut milk can be purchased in tins. It can also be made by grating the white flesh of a coconut, soaked in warm water and strained.

# DRIED FISH & MUSHROOM STEW

*Preparation Time:* 10 minutes
*Cooking Time:* 30 minutes
*Serves:* 4 people

There are different varieties of mushrooms found in Nigeria but the commonly eaten ones have a meaty texture and hardier than most of the mushrooms found in Europe. Due to their natural smoky and delicate aroma and flavour, they are known to enhance the overall taste of the dishes in which they are used. This dish is common in the Ekiti areas of Nigeria.
*Native name(s): Obe olubeje*

*500g of mushrooms, wash & cut into quarters •*
*4 medium tomatoes or 1 tin of plum tomatoes •*
*1 small onion •*
*1 small yellow scotch bonnet, remove seeds, (optional) •*
*200g dried fish (catfish). Soak fish in salted hot water for about 5 minutes, Remove fins and bones. Break into small pieces (smoked haddock or cod can be used instead)•*
*1 tablespoon of locust beans or 1 dadawa cube, (optional) •*
*2 seasoning cube •*
*100ml of palm oil •*
*Handful of finely sliced spinach leaves for garnishing •*

**1** Coarsely blend tomatoes, scotch bonnet (if using) and onions. Heat palm oil in a pot and add blend. Add a cup of water and cook for about 5 minutes under high heat.

**2** Turn heat down and simmer for about 10 minutes. Add locust beans (if using), seasoning cubes, and pinch of salt.

**3** Add dried fish pieces and a cup of hot water. Cover and simmer until the dried fish is just soft. Add mushrooms. Finally add a handful of chopped spinach leaves. Stir well, simmer for 3-5 minutes.

**4** Serve with boiled rice or pounded yam.

**Cook's note**
Caution; spicy recipe, but use of chilli is optional.

Vegetarian option:
prepare meal without dried fish.

African mushrooms may be difficult to source. Some dried ones are available in African food markets. Any preferred variety of mushrooms can be used for this recipe.

Fish & Seafood

43

# BAKED TILAPIA
# WITH SWEET PEPPERS

*Preparation Time:* 10 minutes
*Cooking Time:* 40 minutes
*Serves:* 4 people

Baking allows fish to be cooked whole without crushing and crumbling which enhances the presentation of this dish.

*2 medium whole tilapia, gut and clean thoroughly. Wash in water with a dash of lemon •*
*½ green pepper, finely dice •*
*½ red pepper, finely dice •*
*½ yellow pepper, finely dice •*
*Fish seasoning •*
*Cooking oil •*

**For the sauce**
*4 medium tomatoes or 1 can of plum tomatoes •*
*½ red pepper •*
*1 small scotch bonnet, remove seeds, optional •*
*1 medium onion •*
*2 seasoning cubes •*
*100ml cooking or blended olive oil •*

**1** Rub whole fish with fish seasoning, brush on some oil and place in an oven dish. Cook in the oven (180, gas mark 4) for about 20 minutes.

**2** Simultaneously blend pepper, onion, tomatoes and scotch bonnet (if using), into a smooth blend. Heat oil in a sauce pan and add blend, 2 cups of water, and seasoning cubes. Allow to boil for about 10-15 minutes.

**3** Remove the fish from the oven and carefully scoop the sauce onto the fish in the dish using a ladle. Spread the finely diced sweet peppers on fish and return to the oven to cook for another 10-15 minutes, or until fish is well cooked.

**4** Serve with boiled rice, hard dough bread, boiled potatoes or yam.

**Cook's note**
Caution; spicy recipe, use of chilli is optional.

*Tilapia falls under the category of oily fish, thus very rich in essential fatty acids.*

Recent research shows that **Tilapia** has the lowest mercury residue of all fish tested including salmon, making it the safest known fish for human consumption.

Fish & Seafood

# OGBONNA

*Preparation Time:* 10 minutes
*Cooking Time:* 30 minutes
*Serves:* 4 people

Use only tender and young okra fingers. Click off tips of okra finger to determine tenderness. Tender okra tips click off easily, older ones are woody and tough.

Popular dish in the eastern parts of Nigeria particularly among the 'Igbos'.

*Ogbonna* soup is made with dried seeds of the bush mangoes and a combination of different meat and fish pieces as well as vegetables.

*Native name(s):* apon.

100g of dried catfish, wash and break into small pieces •
15 okra fingers, wash, remove stalk & slice •
A handful of freshly chopped basil •
3 seasoning cubes •
1 cup of beef stock •
½ medium onion, finely chop •
1 small tomato, finely chop •
½ teaspoon of cameroon pepper (very hot but aromatic) or ground dried pepper, optional •
100ml palm oil •
2 tablespoons ground crayfish or 1 crayfish seasoning cube •
1 sliced chunk of stockfish, soak in salted hot water overnight then boil until soft. Break into small pieces (optional) •
4 tablespoons of ground 'ogbonna' seeds •
A handful of fresh prawns •

**1** Heat palm oil in a pot, add finely diced onions and tomato. Fry until browned then add 1 litre of water and allow to boil. Now add cameroun pepper, if using, ground crayfish and seasoning cubes. Stir. Add stock, dried fish, stockfish pieces, if using, cover and bring to the boil. Taste for salt. Allow to boil for 5 minutes.

**2** With a mallet or empty bottle, break down the ground 'ogbonna' lumps to get an even flow grainy powder. Then turn the heat down and add the ground 'ogbonna' a little at time with constant stirring. 'Ogbonna' acts as a thickener so you would need to stir well to avoid lumps developing. Allow to cook and bubble for about 3 minutes.

**3** Add the fresh prawns and okra slices, stir carefully and allow to cook for further 2-3 minutes. Add the fresh basil last. Cover and let simmer for another 1-2 minutes. Dust on more ground crayfish as desired. If required, add some hot water to adjust consistency and simmer until served.

**4** Serve hot with pounded yam or *fufu*.

*Ogbonna* seeds are categorised as oil seeds and are rich in oil soluble vitamins & minerals.

Vegetarian option:
substitute fish and meat pieces with wild mushrooms or more vegetables like *ugwu*.

**Cook's note**
The more 'ogbonna' used, the thicker the soup. Add a spoonful at a time until you achieve your preferred consistency. Use of chilli is optional.

CHAPTER 3

# SOUPS, STEWS & SAUCES

There is a range of soups, stews and sauces common to Nigerian cuisine. These terms are sometimes used interchangeably because of the similarities in their starting ingredients and methods of cooking.

*'scent pepper' Aromatic Green chilli*

Stews are more versatile in Nigerian cuisine. They accompany many other dishes, and can be prepared using a variety of ingredients. The typical Nigerian household will always have some stew stored away in the kitchen, as it is the basis on which most other dishes are made. Stews are made with tomatoes, sweet peppers, onions and fresh chillis. Meats or fish are also added.

Soups and sauces are richer and incorporate essences of vegetables, nuts, barks, pods, roots and sometimes fruits.

# MELON SEEDS & SPINACH STEW

*Preparation Time:* **10 minutes**
*Cooking Time:* **30 minutes**
*Serves:* **4 people**

Melon seeds are used to create one of Nigeria's most popular dishes. Methods of cooking this dish vary by region. The *'Igbos'* use more of melon seeds in this recipe while the *'Yourbas'* use more vegetables. Both methods result in a great tasting dish.

*Native name(s): egusi, agushi*

- *200g of ground melon (pumpkin) seeds*
- *1 large onion, cut into quarters*
- *3 large tomatoes*
- *1 small yellow scotch bonnet, remove seeds (optional)*
- *50g smoked haddock. Cut into bite size pieces*
- *50g of stockfish (optional). Soak stockfish in salty water overnight, and boil until soft and tender. Remove fins & bones. Break into small pieces*
- *150ml palm oil*
- *2 bunches fresh spinach. Wash and pick leaves, shred coarsely*
- *2 seasoning cubes*
- *1 cup of chicken stock*
- *1 small red onion. Finely chop*
- *1 tablespoon locust beans, wash or 1 dadawa cube (optional)*
- *2 tablespoons ground smoked crayfish or 1 crayfish seasoning cube*

**1** Coarsely blend the scotch bonnet (if using), large onion, locust beans (if using), and tomatoes. Pour blend in a sauce pan, add 1 cup of stock and allow to boil for about 10 minutes.

**2** In the meantime, add half a cup of warm water to the ground melon seeds in a bowl and mix into a paste. Heat palm oil in a pot until it starts to smoke. Carefully add the finely chopped red onion and add the melon paste in little scoops. Allow to fry stirring continuously. Add 1 crushed seasoning cube.

**3** Slowly add boiling sauce from step 1 to the frying melon. Stir carefully and add 2 cups of warm water. Add ground smoked crayfish, smoked haddock and stockfish pieces. Allow to cook for about 10 minutes under low heat. Add spinach and second seasoning cube. Stir slowly and taste for salt.

**4** Serve with pounded yam.

Soups Stews & Sauces

Pumpkins or melon seeds are highly nutritious; they are rich in good fats, and are a good source of omega 3 & 6, essential fats needed for hormone balance, brain function and skin health. Also rich in zinc.

### Cook's note
A variety of leafy vegetbles such as *ugwu*, *efo* or bitter leaves can also be used. Smoked mackrel may be used instead of haddock.

Vegetarian option:
prepare meal without smoked haddock or stockfish.

# GUINEA FOWL IN MIXED VEGETABLE SOUP

*Preparation Time:* 20 minutes
*Cooking Time:* 30 minutes
*Serves:* 4 people

Ugwu leaves are grouped as dark leaves vegetables.

Rich in vitamin C and minerals particularly iron.

This dish is popular with the *Efik* people of Southern Nigeria and is a delicacy seen as nutritionally rich. This dish is so good, it is cooked by wives to appease an angry husband.
Traditionally made with pumpkin leaves (*ugwu*), waterleaves and a combination of different varieties of fish and meat pieces. *Ukazi* leaves may also be used.

*Native name(s): edikang-ikang*

*1 medium size guinea fowl (or chicken), cut into bite size pieces, wash •*
*1 bunch ugwu (pumpkin) leaves, wash and pick leaves, finely slice leaves including some tender stalk •*
*1 bunch of spinach. Wash & pick leaves, finely slice •*
*1 bunch of waterleaves (watercress or lambs lettuce may be used as alternatives). Wash & pick leaves, finely slice •*
*1 medium onion, finely chop •*
*6 medium fresh tomatoes, wash & finely chop •*
*50g of stockfish. Soak in salted water over night. Then boil until soft for about 1½ hours, remove bones and break into small pieces •*
*A handful of smoked prawns, remove head and tail, shell and wash. Soak in hot water for 5 minutes, drain •*
*1 scotch bonnet remove stalk & seeds, finely chop •*
*100-150ml of palm oil •*
*1 cup chicken stock •*
*2 tablespoons of ground crayfish •*
*2 seasoning cubes •*

1 Heat oil in a pot and add chopped onions and scotch bonnet, fry for 1 minute, then add the guinea fowl pieces. Stir fry to seal juices. Add seasoning cubes, chopped tomatoes. Stir well.

2 Add stock and stockfish and cook for 5 minutes. Add 2 cups of hot water and the ground crayfish, stir and allow to simmer for another few minutes, taste for salt.

3 Add the '*ugwu*' leaves, stir and allow to simmer for 2 minutes. Then add spinach leaves and stir. Finally add the smoked prawns pieces cover pot and simmer for 1-2 minutes. Add the waterleaves last. Stir well then simmer for another 2 minutes.

4 Serve with pounded yam.

> **Cook's note**
> Chicken, goat meat or beef may be used for this dish. Caution; spicy recipe, use of chilli is optional.

Vegetarian option: prepare meal without guinea fowl, fish & smoked prawns.

# TUWO & GROUNDNUT SOUP

*Preparation Time:* 10 minutes
*Cooking Time:* 30 minutes
*Serves:* 2-3 people

This dish is popular in the northern regions of Nigeria. '*Tuwo*' which accompanies the groundnut soup can be made using a variety of grains including sorghum, millet and rice.

*Native name(s): tuwo d'miya gyada*

*2-3 tablespoons of groundnut paste or smooth peanut butter* •
*1 medium onion* •
*6 tomatoes, wash & chop* •
*300g of chicken breast, wash and cut into bite size pieces* •
*½ red sweet pepper* •
*100ml of groundnut oil* •
*1 sprig fresh thyme* •
*2 seasoning cubes* •
*Thinly sliced chives* •
*½ scotch bonnet (optional), remove seeds* •
*3 cups of long grain or basmati rice* •

1 Season chicken pieces with thyme, 1 seasoning cube and salt. Boil for 5 minutes. Remove chicken pieces and set aside on a plate. Sieve chicken stock and retain for use in step 2.

2 Blend pepper, scotch bonnet (if using), tomatoes and onion into a smooth blend. Heat oil in a pot and add blend. Add 750ml water and cook for 15 minutes. Add the ground groundnut paste. Stir carefully to evenly dissolve paste. Add second seasoning cube and taste for salt. Add the chicken pieces and allow to cook for 5 minutes under low heat.

3 Check consistency and add 1 cup of hot water, more if required. Simmer. Garnish with chives.

4 Simultaneously boil rice, adding a pinch of salt, until very soft. When rice becomes soft to the touch, mash up by continuously stirring with a wooden spoon. Then mould as desired. Serve with the groundnut soup.

Groundnuts are also called peanuts. This recipe should be avoided by those allergic to nuts. Groundnuts are rich in protein, fat soluble vitamins (A & D) and minerals like zinc and potassium.

Cook's note
The best result will be achieved if *tuwo* is made using rice with high starch content (sticky rice).
Use of chilli is optional.

Vegetarian option:
substitute chicken with mushrooms
and other vegetables of choice.

# MELON SEED SOUP & EWEDU

*Preparation Time:* 10 minutes
*Cooking Time:* 40 minutes
*Serves:* 4 people

The Yoruba word *ewedu* translates as 'dark leaf'. It falls under the category of dark green leaf vegetables promising same degree of nutrients and goodness.

4 fillets of red bream, wash, rub with some salt and set aside •
2 bunches of ewedu leaves. Pick leaves off the stalks & wash thoroughly, then allow to drain from a colander •
3 seasoning cubes •
1 spoon of washed locust beans or 1 dadawa cube (optional) •
2 tablespoons of dried ground crayfish •
1 cup melon or pumpkin seeds, wash •
4 ripe fresh tomatoes or 1 tin of plum tomatoes •
1 small yellow scotch bonnet, (optional), remove seeds and stalk •
1 onion •

1 Place *ewedu* leaves in a blender with 1 cup of water*. Blend leaves finely. Dissolve 1 seasoning cube in 1 cup of water in a small pot. When boiled, add the blended *ewedu* leaves, stir well and boil for about 5 minutes. Add ground crayfish. Stir and allow to cook for a further 2-3 minutes, stirring continuously to avoid bubbling and boiling over. Turn heat off and set aside.

2 Simultaneously, finely blend melon seeds, tomatoes, onion and scotch bonnet (if using) together. Heat palm oil in a pot, add blend, 500ml of water and bring to boil for about 15 minutes. Add 2 seasoning cubes. Stir and simmer under low heat until served.

3 Pan fry red bream fillets 4-5 minutes on each side.

4 Dish *ewedu* and melon seeds soups, place fish on top and serve with *amala*. Can also be served with pounded yam or *fufu*.

### Cook's note
*When blending the *ewedu* leaves start by blending a few (about a hand full) leaves in 1 cup of water, then increasingly add more until all leaves have been added. More water may be added to aid blending. Continue until you achieve a fine blend. Use of chilli is optional.

Ewedu leaves are also known as jute leaves. Grouped under dark leaves vegetables, they are rich in iron and vitamin B6.

Vegetarian option: prepare recipe without fish.

# BANGA SOUP

This is a classic soup popular across West Africa. Made from raw palm kernels and delicate aromatic spices (*ataieko* and *iregaegie*) which provide its distinct taste and flavour. Also known as palm-nut soup.

*Preparation Time:* **10 minutes**
*Cooking Time:* **50 minutes**
*Serves:* **4 people**

1 400g tin of palm kernel soup base •
1 large fresh red bream, clean with a splash of lemon juice and slice into 4 thick steaks •
½ onion •
½ red pepper •
1 cup of stock •
2 seasoning cubes •
2 serving spoons smoked ground crayfish •
1 teaspoon ground ginger, 1 teaspoon black pepper, a pinch of ground cloves •
Fresh basil, finely chop •

Palm Kernels

1 Blend pepper and onion. Transfer blend into a large sauce pan. Add the stock, stir and allow to boil for 5 minutes.

2 Empty the tin of palm kernel soup base into the boiling sauce and stir well. Then add the, ginger and black pepper (or a spoon or 2 of pepper soup mix can be used instead). Add 2 cups of water, stir, cover the pan and slow cook for about 25 minutes for the flavours to develop.

3 Gently un-cover the pan and stir. Add the seasoning cubes and the ground crayfish. Lastly add the fish steaks. Simmer for another 5 minutes, or until fish is cooked.

4 Garnish with a handful of finely chopped basil and serve hot with boiled yams or boiled ripe plantain. If cooked with okra slices, *Banga* soup can be served with pounded yam.

### Cook's note
There are different variaions of *Banga* soup. A range of meats, dried or fresh fish, and vegetable (eg okra) can be added. The key ingredient is the palm kernal base which provides the distint flavour and aroma. Equally important are the spices. Pepper soup mix can be used to create a more traditional taste.

# GREEN PEPPER SAUCE

Vegetarian option: substitute meat with mushrooms

*Ofada*, Nigerians' main cultivated rice is back on the menu because of its increasing nutritional profile. It is delicious and easy to cook. Best served with green pepper sauce.

*Native name(s): aya mase, designer stew*

*Preparation Time:* 10 minutes
*Cooking Time:* 45 minutes
*Serves:* 2-3 people

2 cups of African 'ofada' rice remove chaffs or stones, wash and drain •
100g beef, trim dice into small pieces & wash •
1 tablespoon locust beans •
1 red onion, finely chop •
1½ large green pepper •
1 scotch bonnet, remove stalk and seeds •
1 seasoning cube •
2 serving spoons vegetable oil, (palm oil is Traditionally used) •
Fresh thyme •

*Ofada rice retains much of its nutrients which other varieties of rice have lost through processes such as polishing.*

**1** Season beef pieces with thyme, 1 seasoning cube, add some water and boil for about 10 minutes. Transfer beef onto a baking tray and grill for another 10 minutes. Save the stock for use in step 2.

**2** Blend scotch bonnet and green pepper with 500ml of water. Heat oil in a sauce pan until it just starts to smoke. Add chopped red onions, add the blend and stir. Add the stock (step 1) cook for about 5 minutes, turn heat down, add the locust beans, meat pieces and simmer to reduce sauce. Taste for salt.

**3** Boil some water and add rice. Cook until tender and drain excess water using a colander. Add salt, and toss.

**4** Serve 'ofada' rice with the sauce. Long grain or basmati rice may also be used in this recipe.

### Cook's note
Hot! The use of scotch bonnet is required for this recipe. Slicing the chilli and adding with the onions in step 2 rather than blending may reduce the heat. Other milder forms of chilli may however be used as a substitute.

Soups Stews & Sauces

CHAPTER 4

# STAPLES & VEGETABLES

*Jute (ewedu) leaves*

There is an abundance of vegetables in Nigeria and they vary from region to region. Vegetables contribute to the staples of particular tribes or locality. Some vegetables are eaten raw and fresh but a wider variety of vegetables are cooked before eating. Some are even cooked and eaten mainly for their medicinal properties (bitter leaves for example). Methods of cooking vegetables include steaming, boiling or stewing.

Some vegetables are dried and powdered for preservation and flavour enhancement. An example is powdered okra which produces *luru* a delicacy in the middle and northern areas of Nigeria. Vegetables are an important part of Nigerian diet because they always accompany the main staples like pounded yam, *fufu*, *amala* and *gari*.

*Cooked jute leaves—ewedu soup*

The use and processing of vegetables vary by region and tribes. It is fascinating to see how same vegetables are processed into different food products or dishes.

Staples across the country are rich in carbohydrates and relied on as the main source of energy.

# EFO RIRO

*Preparation Time:* 10 minutes
*Cooking Time:* 30 minutes
*Serves:* 4 people

*4 bunches of broad leaves spinach, wash.*
*Pick leaves with a bit of tender stalk,*
*shred* •
*6 medium fresh tomatoes* •
*1 medium onion* •
*1 yellow scotch bonnet, optional* •
*1 tablespoon locust beans or 1 dadawa cube,*
*optional* •
*4 fish cutlets (any white fish), wash and*
*remove bone* •
*2 tablespoons ground crayfish* •
*1 cup of chicken stock* •
*50g smoked haddock (or smoked mackerel).*
*Cut into small pieces* •
*150ml palm oil* •
*2 seasoning cubes* •

A typical Yoruba dish. This dish is a quick and simple way to prepare and enjoy fresh, green and leafy vegetables.

**1** Boil 2 cups of water, dissolve a seasoning cube add blanch spinach for no more that 1 minute. Drain and allow to rest. Alternatively, place spinach leaves in a food bag, and blanch in the microwave for 1-2 minutes.

**2** Coarsely blend onion, tomatoes, scotch bonnet (if using), and locust beans. Heat palm oil in a pot and add blend. Add stock and stir. Allow to boil for about 10 minutes, then add ground crayfish and continue to cook. Check salt. Add the fish cutlets and allow to cook for another 5 minutes, then add the smoked haddock, stir, also add 1 seasoning cube. Then add the blanched spinach. Stir well to mix sauce with spinach. Cover and simmer for another 2-3 minutes or till the fish is cooked.

**3** Best served with pounded yam but can also be served with rice, *amala, gari* etc

**Cook's note**
Caution; spicy recipe, use of chilli is optional.

Vegetarian option: cook without fish or substitute with mushrooms.

Fresh green vegetables such as spinach, ugwu, tete, soko, etc., contain a range of B complex vitamins, and minerals like iron and magnesium.

*Vegetables & Staples*

# YAM POTTAGE WITH PAN FRIED HAKE

*Preparation Time:* 10 minutes
*Cooking Time:* 30 minutes
*Serves:* 4 people

Yam pottage is a nutritionally complete dish. *Puna* yam or white yam are best used for this recipe due to their naturally sweet and creamy properties.

Native name(s): *ebe, asaro*

½ tuber of 'puna' yam. Peel off skin, cut into large cubed chunks (see picture) and wash •
1 tablespoon tomato puree (optional) •
100ml palm oil •
1 seasoning cube •
1 large red onion. Cut into quarters •
2 tomatoes •
Chives, finely chop •
2 tablespoons of ground crayfish •
4 cutlets of hake, remove skin and bones, wash •
1 large tomato. Cut into quarters •
½ red sweet pepper •
1 teaspoon cameroun pepper (optional) •
1 tablespoon of Sugar (optional) •
1 litre water •

**1** Coarsely blend tomatoes, onions and pepper in a blender. Transfer blend into a large pot and bring to the boil. Add seasoning cube, tomato puree if using, water and cameroun pepper if using. Cook for about 5 minutes.

**2** Simultaneously toss yam chunks with salt and briskly deep fry for no more than 1 minute in very hot oil. This step is optional but helps to retain the shape of the yam cubes.

**3** Carefully place yam cubes, into the sauce (step1), add 2 cups of hot water and cover, also add sugar if using. Cook under low heat until yam chunks become soft. Stir gently taking care not to crush all the yam cubes. Some will by now be crushed into a smooth creamy paste. Add oil and ground crayfish. Mix carefully and simmer for a further 5 minutes. Garnish with chopped chives or spring onions.

**4** Simultaneously pan fry hake for about 3 minutes on each side depending on their thickness. Sprinkle some salt and serve with pottage immediately.

---

**Cook's note**
Palm oil may be substituted with other preferred vegetable oils. Use of chilli is optional.

Vegetarian option:
prepare recipe without using fish.

Palm oil defines the colour of this recipe. Pure, unadulterated palm oil is rich in essential fatty acids and vitamins A & E. Yams are a good source of energy minerals and vitamin C. They ensure a steady supply of energy.

*Vegetables & Staples*

# ESSENTIAL ACCOMPANIMENTS

**◄Fried plantain**
Prepared by deep frying plantain and served with rice or bean dishes. Also eaten with stews or soups. Native name: *dodo*

**Chipped Yam►**
Prepared by deep frying yam pieces. Often served with bean dishes or fried fish, with stews or in soups. Native name: *dundu*.

**▼Rice & Beans**
Eaten widely and regularly, and nutritionally complete. Proportion of rice and beans used depends on preference. To prepare wash beans and rice separately then, boil beans first in some salted water. Add rice when beans are almost cooked. Continue to cook until both become soft. Usually served with stews or sauces.

**▼African Rice (*ofada*)**
Once regarded as inferior rice, *ofada* has become very popular and now valued for its nutritional benefits. It has character and a delicate taste which is desirable. To prepare, boil some water, add the washed rice grains to cook. When soft, turn into a colander to drain excess water, add salt and toss. Popularly served with green pepper sauce. (pg 58)

**▼Steamed White Rice**
Most common staple, eaten on all occasions. Nigerians eat different varieties of rice such as long grain or broken rice, and more recently basmati rice. Rice can be boiled or steamed and eaten with stews or sauces. It can also be mashed up into *tuwo* or cooked with other vegetables like beans or peas.

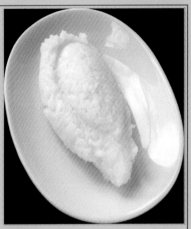

### ◄Pounded Yam
Undoubtedly the most popular accompaniment to many vegetable soups. Traditionally prepared by boiling and pounding yam in a large mortar with pestles.

Pounded yam flour has been developed to simplify its preparation. The yam flour is simply added to hot water and stirred into a smooth paste.

Pounded yam can also be made in a micro wave oven, by mixing yam flour with cold water in a bowl. The emergent loose mixture is micro-waved for between 5-10 minutes, removing and stirring frequently. Adjust amount of flour or water as desired.

Electronic pounding machines or high voltage food processors can also be used to make pounded yam from boiled yam slices.

### Semolina/Ground rice
Modern variations of *foofoo*. Prepared by adding semolina granules or ground rice to hot water and stirring until a moderately soft and smooth paste is produced.

### Eko Tutu, Agidi
This is one staple that is preferred eaten cold! Made from *Ogi* (see page 96) or *pap*. The ogi paste or powder is dissolved in some water. Hot water is poured over to form a gel which is boiled for a few minutes and allowed to cool and set. Eaten with vegetable stews, *akara* or *moin-moin*.

### ▲Tuwo
Popular staple eaten by the northerners. Made from rice which is boiled until soft and mashed up. *Tuwo* can also be made from other grains such as millet, corn & sorghum. Served with 'miya kuka' or groundnut soup (pg 54).

### Akpu, Fufu
Popular in the east. Made from fermented cassava and sold as a ready meal, wrapped in leaves. Also made from *fufu* flour by stirring into warm (70c) water and cooking over high heat into a smooth paste.

### Hard Dough Bread
Eaten with stews, soups and bean dishes. Also eaten with fried eggs/omelettes for breakfast.

### ▼Cassava Granules-Garri
Product of fermented and fried grated cassava. There are two varieties, white and yellow. Prepared by boiling water, carefully adding the *gari* granules, and stirring until a moderately soft and smooth paste is achieved. Eaten with different types of vegetable soups.
*Native name*(s): *gari, eba*

### Yam Flour►
More popular in western Nigeria. *Amala* can be made from cassava flour (*lafun*), plantain flour or yam flour. Making *amala* requires experience and skill to avoid lumps developing. To prepare, boil some water and turn off the heat. Add sieved yam flour a cup at a time and stir to form a soft doughy mass. Continue to add flour until the right consistency is achieved. The process requires constant stirring and further cooking under high heat for a few minutes. This is followed by a pulling technique to aerate and improve texture. Typically served with *ewedu*. Also served with other vegetable soups. *Native name(s): amala*.

# BOILED YAM WITH OMELETTE

*Preparation Time:* 5 minutes
*Cooking Time:* 5 minutes
*Serves:* 3 people

- *3 raw king prawns, wash and de-vein. Cut into small bits*
- *6 medium sized eggs*
- *¼ medium size onion, finely dice*
- *¼ sweet red pepper, finely dice*
- *¼ sweet green pepper, finely dice*
- *½ seasoning cube*
- *1 teaspoon of tomato paste (1 tablespoon of leftover stew or pepper sauce may also be used)*
- *3 medium slices of puna (or white) yam, wash*
- *50ml cooking oil*
- *¼ cup of fresh milk or Water*
- *Salt and sugar*

**1** Boil yam in a pot, add a pinch of salt and 1 teaspoon of sugar. When cooked, drain excess water, cover and set aside.

**2** Simultaneously whisk eggs in a bowl and add milk. Mix tomato paste with 2–3 tablespoons of water and add to eggs. Mix well. Also add crushed seasoning cube and pinch of salt to taste. Whisk all together. Finally add onions, peppers and prawns. Mix well.

**3** Heat oil in a large frying pan, pour whisked eggs, fry for 1 minute and turn down heat. Turn eggs over to cook other side. Allow to cook for another 2-3 minutes. Serve with yam slices.

Yams are full of minerals and vitamin C. They also ensure a constant supply of (slow release) energy.

# SCRAMBLED EGGS WITH HARDDOUGH BREAD

Eggs were rarely eaten in the olden times because they were rather left to hatch into chickens!

Nowadays, they are eaten boiled, scrambled or as omelettes. Boiled eggs are sometimes cooked in stews in place of meat.

*Preparation Time:* 10 minutes
*Cooking Time:* 5 minutes
*Serves:* 3 people

6 medium eggs •
1 small onion, finely dice •
3 small ripe tomatoes, finely dice •
1 scotch bonnet, remove seeds and finely dice (optional) •
1 seasoning cube •
Hard dough bread •
100ml cooking oil •

**1** In a large frying pan, heat the oil, add the onions and tomatoes, stir well. Then add half a cup of water, cook until tomatoes and onions are soft. Then add seasoning cube. Stir well.

**2** Simultaneously whisk eggs in a bowl and add pinch of salt to taste. Add eggs to the frying onions and tomatoes. Scramble eggs in the pan and fry for 2-3 minutes or until well cooked. Finally add diced scotch bonnet (if using) and stir in.

**3** Slice the hard dough bread, butter and toast as desired, serve with eggs.

# AFRICAN BEANS WITH SWEETCORN

*Preparation Time:* 10 minutes
*Cooking Time:* 30 minutes
*Serves:* 2 people

*500g of African brown beans (oloyin beans), pick stones & wash •*
*1 small onions •*
*2 large tomatoes •*
*1 teaspoon ground chilli powder (optional) •*
*1 350g can of sweet corn, drain water (or 200g 0f frozen sweet corn) •*
*100ml of palm oil •*
*1 litre of water •*
*Salt and sugar •*

1 Boil beans in a pressure cooker without placing the lid in the first instance. Coarsely blend the tomatoes and onion and add to beans. Also add 1 seasoning cube, chilli powder if using, cover the pressure cooker and boil under pressure for 15 minutes or until beans become soft to the touch.

2 Remove pressure cooker from heat and open carefully. Using a wooden spoon carefully stir beans. Then add sweet corn to the beans. Stir well. Add salt and 2 table spoons of sugar or more if preferred. Stir well.

3 Turn down heat and add the palm oil. Add about half a cup of hot water to adjust the consistency. Cover and simmer for a further 10 minutes stirring occasionally. Serve hot.

> **Cook's note**
> Cook beans in a pressure cooker to significantly reduce cooking time.

70

**1** Wash and place garden eggs in a small pot and boil in water for about 10 minutes under moderate heat. Remove garden eggs and place in cold water to cool. Then carefully remove skin and place in a separate plate.

**2** Heat oil in a sauce pan and add onions and tomatoes. Crumble the seasoning cube and add. Add 2 serving spoons of water and stir well. Taste for salt. Allow to simmer for 3-5 minutes. Add the egg plants, and mash slightly. Stir well into the sauce and simmer for further 3 minutes. Add spring onions and stir.

**3** Simultaneously boil yam with a pinch of salt until soft, serve with egg plant stew, garnished with cooked prawns.

# EGG PLANT STEW

Garden eggs are round shiny vegetables usually white and egg shaped. They can be eaten raw, they have a pleasant but slightly bitter taste. They can also be cooked in stews and used in salads.

Believed to be rich in vitamins and minerals which promote good health. Garden eggs belong to the same family as aubergines.

*Preparation Time:* 10 minutes
*Cooking Time:* 20 minutes
*Serves:* 3 people

- *6 small garden eggs*
- *1 onion, slice*
- *3 tomatoes, chop*
- *1 seasoning cube*
- *100ml palm oil*
- *12 cooked prawns*
- *3 slices of puna yam*
- *1 stalk of spring onion slice to garnish*

Garden eggs are rich in minerals such as magnesium and vitamin C.

 Suitable for vegetarians when served without prawns.

# OKRA SOUP

*Preparation Time:* 10 minutes
*Cooking Time:* 20 minutes
*Serves:* 3 people

Okra soup is also known as gumbo in parts of North America and West Indies. It is one of the most eaten soups in Nigeria.

Quick and easy to prepare, this soup can be eaten with a variety of other dishes, in particular pounded yam or *gari*. There are different variations of this soup as we move across the nation, with the use of a variety of meat, fish and other vegetables such as *ugwu*, bitter leaves etc.

*Native name(s): ila asepo*

*20 okra fingers (about 200g), wash, remove stalk and cut into thick slices •*
*3 hake medium sized cutlets, wash •*
*1 medium tomato, finely dice •*
*¼ medium size onion, finely dice •*
*1 teaspoon cameroun pepper or ground dried chilli, optional •*
*1 seasoning cube •*
*2 tablespoons ground crayfish or 1 crayfish seasoning cube •*
*1 tablespoon locust beans or 1 dadawa cube (optional) •*
*75ml of palm oil •*

**1** Heat oil in a pot and fry diced tomatoes and onions until browned. Add about 500ml of water, cameroun pepper, seasoning cube, locust beans and ground crayfish. Allow to boil for about 3-5 minutes.

**2** Now add fish cutlets and cook for a further 3-5 minutes. Turn heat down and carefully add the sliced okra. Add salt to taste and some hot water to adjust consistency. Simmer for 1-2 minutes.

**3** Serve hot, with pounded yam, *gari*, *fufu*, *amala*, or semolina

**Cook's note**
Any preferred fish can be used for this dish. Caution; spicy recipe, use of chilli is optional. To reduce okra slime, sautee sliced okra in oil for about 2 minutes before adding to cooking.

Vegetarian option:
substitute fish with mushrooms.

*Okra fingers are a good source of many nutrients including vitamins B6 & C. also rich in fibre, calcium and folates.*

Vegetables & Staples

# JOLLOF RICE

**Preparation Time:** 10 minutes
**Cooking Time:** 30 minutes
**Serves:** 4 people

### Cook's note
Caution; spicy recipe but use of chilli is optional. To reduce chilli heat but get its flavour, add whole chilli to cooking and remove before serving. You may prewash rice in warm water before cooking depending on brand used. Easycook rice is best for this recipe.

Contrary to general belief, *'jollof'* rice did not originate from Nigeria but rather from the Wolof people of Senegal and Gambia. However, Nigerians are the highest consumers of *'jollof'* rice. It is an important festive meal.

There are many variations of *'jollof'* rice but all contain common basic ingredients which include fresh tomatoes, onions, chilli, red peppers and tomato paste. Thyme, curry powder and bay leaf are desirable spices that are also used.

3 cups (750g) easy cook basmati rice •
4 large plum tomatoes or 1 can of plum tomatoes •
1 tablespoon tomato puree •
5 sprigs of fresh thyme •
2 teaspoon freshly milled or ground nutmeg •
1 cup chicken stock •
1 medium size onion •
4 seasoning cubes •
1 scotch bonnet (yellow). Remove stalk & seeds, finely chop (optional) •
1 large sweet red pepper. Remove stalk & seeds •
3 serving spoons of butter or margarine •
freshly chopped chives •
1 crayfish seasoning cube or 1 tablespoon of ground crayfish •
A small piece of ginger or 1 teaspoon ground ginger •
1 teaspoon curry powder •
1 serving spoon vegetable oil •

Fresh thyme and ground nutmeg enhance the taste of this dish.

Vegetarian option:
Serve without beef or chicken.
Avoid use of chicken stock.

**1** Blend the tomatoes, sweet pepper and onion together. Pour blend in a large pot, then add the scotch bonnet, thyme, nutmeg, curry powder, crayfish cube and chicken stock. Also add 750ml of water. Bring to the boil. Pound or grate the ginger and add to the boiling mix. Stir slowly, add tomato puree and allow to boil for about 5 minutes under high heat.

**2** Turn heat down, slowly introduce rice and stir in. Add some hot water enough to cook the rice, cover pot first with a sheet of foil paper and then with the pot lid. Allow to steam for about 10 minutes.

**3** Open pot and check if rice is cooked. Add more hot water if required. When all water/moisture has evaporated, gently stir rice avoiding scraping the bottom of the pot, also avoid overcooking rice. Crush and sprinkle seasoning cubes, stir well to distribute seasoning, then taste for salt, (use more or less seasoning cube depending on preference). Add two serving spoons of butter and mix well. Also add a serving spoon of vegetable oil to give the desirable glister.

**4** Serve hot with fried meat, fish or grilled chicken. Garnish with chives.

Vegetables & Staples

# FRIED RICE

*Preparation Time:* 10 minutes
*Cooking Time:* 30 minutes
*Serves:* 2 people

This is another popular rice dish which incorporates the use of vegetables and an assortment of meat or fish pieces.
Often prepared for festive occasions along with *jollof* rice.

- *1 small carrot, finely dice*
- *¼ green pepper, finely dice*
- *¼ yellow pepper*
- *1 small onion, dice*
- *1 handful frozen green peas*
- *1 teaspoon curry powder*
- *1 sprig of fresh thyme or 1 teaspoon of dried thyme*
- *1 handful shrimps or prawns, wash & de-vein*
- *2 cups of easy cook basmati rice, wash & drain*
- *1 cup of chicken stock*
- *2 seasoning cube*
- *100ml cooking or blended olive oil*

1 Boil rice in chicken stock until just soft. Allow to cool for about 10 minutes.

2 In a large pan or wok, heat oil, and stir fry the onion, carrot and peas. Add curry powder and thyme. Continue to stir fry. Then add green peppers and simmer adding a sprinkling of water.

3 Add the rice to the frying vegetables one spoon at a time and stir well. Add the prawns last, cover to simmer for 2-3 minutes under high heat. Crush the seasoning cube and sprinkle over the rice. Also add 2 hand sprinklings of water. Stir fry for a further 1 minute. Taste for salt.

4 Serve hot with grilled spicy chicken.

Vegetarian option:
substitute prawns with mushrooms or other vegetables of choice.

**Cook's note**
A range of meat and vegetable pieces can be used and is not limited to what has been used for this recipe. Proportion of vegetables used should depend on personal preference.

*vegetables & staples*

CHAPTER 5

# SNACKS, DESSERTS & DRINKS

Desserts are increasingly becoming appealing to the Nigerian adult, compared to the past where kids were the only ones interested in sweets and puddings.

More common are fresh fruits eaten between meals or used to make different desserts and drinks like salads, smoothies and punches.

A variety of snacks are eaten as comfort foods and these include those served with some dipping sauces or made into chips or crisps.

*Palm wine and suya*

*Ojojo rings*

There is a variety of local brews and drinks made from grains such as sorghum, millet and corn. These include *burukutu, otin'ka, pito, ogogoro* to mention a few. There are also dairy based drinks such as *nono* (taken with *fura*) and *kunu*.

Naturally occurring drinks from plants also form part of meals particularly in the regions where these drinks are readily available. From the palm tree for instance there is fresh coconut water, coconut milk and palm juice or palm wine.

# BEAN FRITTERS SERVED IN A BUN

*Preparation Time:* 50 minutes
*Cooking Time:* 15 minutes
*Serves:* 4 people

A reference to Nigerian cuisine influencing other cuisines of the world. In Brazil, this recipe is called *acaraje*. Bean fritters make a hearty snack or light meal and quite nutritious too.

*Native name(s) kosai, akara*

2 cups of brown African beans (oloyin) •
1 tomato •
1 teaspoon tomato paste •
2 small onions •
Shrimps •
Spring onions, thinly slice •
2 seasoning cubes •
1 egg •
1 tablespoons of ground crayfish •
Burger buns •
Water cress •
Palm oil or vegetable oil for frying •

**1** Soak beans in water for 30 minutes. Then rub soaked beans together to peel skin and reveal the white bean shells. Discard bean skin. Blend inner bean shells, onions and tomato in a blender. Add water to assist blending. Transfer blend to a mixing bowl and with a wooden spoon, mix for about 2 minutes continuously. Dissolve the seasoning cubes in some hot water (2-3 tablespoons) and add to mixture. Add the tomato paste. Mix. Whisk egg and add. Mix for a further 1-2 minutes. Add shrimps and sliced spring onions. Mix.

**2** Scoop dollops of mixture into hot palm oil or preferred vegetable oil and fry for about 2 minutes or until golden brown. Mop excess oil using a kitchen towel.

**3** To make the sauce, finely dice 1 small tomato, ¼ of red and yellow sweet peppers. Sauté in 50ml of oil, add ½ seasoning cube and 1 tablespoon of ground smoked crayfish.

**4** Serve bean fritter in a bun and garnish with watercress and sauce.

*Snacks, Desserts & Drinks*

> **Cook's note**
> ▸ Soaking the beans softens them and easier to blend. For best results blend beans into a fine smooth paste. This can be achieved from a continuous blast of the blender. Bean flour may also be used for this recipe but the result may differ.

# OJOJO RINGS

*Preparation Time:* 20 minutes
*Cooking Time:* 15 minutes
*Serves:* 4 people

- *500g of water yam*
- *1 small onion, finely chop*
- *1 seasoning cube*
- *1 okra finger (optional)*
- *Shrimps, thinly slice*

**Cook's note:** *Ojojo* is often deep fried in dollops but this could make them too greasy. Fry them in smaller pieces which will cook quickly to avoid them becoming oil drenched. Also drain properly using kitchen towels after frying.

**1** Peel yam and wash. Finely grate using the finest side of a grater. Also grate the okra finger if using. Crush the seasoning cube and add to the grated yam.

**2** Using bare hands mix thoroughly. Add onion and shrimps and mix again thoroughly. Fry a small sample dollop to check for salt. Add more salt if necessary.

**3** Using an extrusion pocket, extrude the mixture into hot oil and deep fry under a moderately high heat. Mop up excess oil using kitchen towel. You can also deep fry in any size dollops or shape as preferred.

**4** Can be eaten alone hot or served with *èko*.

# YAM CHIPS

Nigeria's equivalent to potato chips. *Dundu* is made by deep frying yams. Can be eaten as a snack or a light evening meal. Usually served with a spicy sauce and fried fish.

*Preparation Time:* 10 minutes
*Cooking Time:* 30 minutes
*Serves:* 3 people

- *500g of puna yam*
- *¼ medium onion*
- *¼ green pepper, finely chop*
- *¼ red pepper, finely chop*

For the dip
- *¼ red pepper*
- *¼ onion*
- *2 ripe tomatoes*
- *50ml cooking oil*
- *1 seasoning cube*
- *1 spoon ground crayfish*

**1** Finely blend tomatoes, ¼ onion and ¼ red pepper. Heat oil in pan and add blend. Add the seasoning cube and simmer for about 10 minutes. Add ground crayfish and mix. Taste for salt. Finally add the finely chopped green & red pepper and onions. Stir in and allow to cook for 2-3 minutes.

**2** Simultaneously peel yam, wash and chip. Sprinkle some salt and deep fry for 2-4 minutes. Drain oil.

**3** Serve with the dip and some fried fish.

# PUFF-PUFF & MAPLE SYRUP

Puff-puff is served to celebrate the birth of a baby. Delicious when served hot. Increasingly served as a starter or snack.

*Preparation Time:* 10 minutes
*Proofing time:* 120 minutes
*Cooking Time:* 10 minutes
*Serves:* 10 people

- ½ *teaspoon of ground nutmeg*
- ½ *teaspoon of ground cinnamon*
- *500g of plain flour*
- *7-10g instant yeast*
- *200g brown sugar (more or less as preferred)*
- *450ml lukewarm water*
- *a pinch of salt (optional)*
- *maple syrup*

**1** Sieve flour to aerate. In a mixing bowl, mix flour, sugar, nutmeg, cinnamon, salt and yeast. Then add warm water a little at a time and mix well. (You may use a hand held mixer). Cover bowl with a tea towel and allow to proof for about 2 hours (depending on the strength of the yeast) in a warm place undisturbed.

**2** Remove the tea towel. The dough should have risen in the bowl. Moving in one direction, swirl dough slightly with bare hands or a scoop spoon. Then deep fry dollops of the dough in very hot oil for about 3-5minutes. Remove and transfer onto a colander or kitchen tissue to drain excess oil.

**3** Dribble some maple syrup and serve hot.

**Cook's note:**
Caution when making the dough, mix well, to ensure you achieve the right or your preferred consistency. Fry *puff-puff* in small dollops to avoid them becoming oil drenched. Also mop up excess oil using kitchen towels after frying.

## SHAPED CHIN-CHIN

*Preparation Time:* 30 minutes
*Cooking Time:* 10 minutes
*Serves:* 4 people

500g of plain flour •
3 tablespoons of unsalted butter or margarine •
1 teaspoon of ground nutmeg •
2 eggs •
300ml fresh milk or water •
200g sugar (more or less as preferred) •
A pinch of salt •

**1** Sieve flour to aerate. In a mixing bowl, mix flour, butter, nutmeg, salt and sugar. Now add whisked egg and milk. Mould into a hard pastry dough. Allow to rest for about 5 minutes.

**2** Turn out onto a floured surface and knead well for about 10 minutes. Dust on more flour as required. You should by now have achieved a hard dough. Roll out into a flat sheet. Cut into your preferred shapes. Dust with more flour and allow to stand for another 5 minutes before frying.

**3** At high temperature, deep fry shaped dough for about 3-5 minutes depending on their thickness. Allow to cool & serve with a cold drink.

**Cook's note:**
*Chin-chin* dough is usually cut into long strips before frying but you can have fun by cutting into any fun shape of choice before frying.

## PLANTAIN CRISPS

**1** Peel plantain and thinly slice across its width. Sprinkle some seasoning salt and toss well to ensure each slice is salted and separated.

**2** Heat palm oil until it starts to smoke and deep fry plantain slices for about 4 minutes.

**3** Drain and serve.

*Preparation Time:* 2 minutes
*Cooking Time:* 20 minutes
*Serves:* 1 person

• 1 green plantain
• Palm oil or preferred vegetable oil
• Seasoning salt

**Cook's note:** the choice of plantain is crucial for this recipe. Mature plantains just beginning to ripen are best for this recipe.

# CHEWY COCONUT CANDY WITH ICE-CREAM

Coconut candy is one of the oldest traditionally made sweets known in Nigeria.

*Preparation Time:* 10 minutes
*Cooking Time:* 30 minutes
*Serves:* 4 people

*1 coconut, shell and retain the coconut water •*
*100g of brown sugar (more or less as preferred ) •*
*4-5 tablespoons maple sauce or honey (more or less as preferred) •*
*2 cups water •*

**1** Break coconut and remove shell. Save the coconut water. Scrape off the brown back of coconut and finely grate the white part using a cheese grater.

**2** Heat 2 cups of water in a pot, add saved coconut water and sugar. Then add the grated coconut flesh. Cook under low-moderate heat, stirring continuously until browned and all the water has been heated off. Add maple syrup. Stir well. Then, while still warm, carefully spoon the emerging coconut candy into your preferred shaper/mould. Set aside to cool. (The candy in this recipe has been made into flat, round biscuit shapes, see picture.)

**3** Serve warm candy with cold with ice-cream.

**1** Remove fish head and gut. Cut into 2-3 cutlets and rinse well. Place fish cutlets in a pot, add 1 seasoning cube and enough water to cook them. Add some fresh thyme and boil until fish is cooked. Remove fish and in a plate remove bones and skin. With a fork, flake the fish. Ensure you remove all specks of bone. Set aside.

**2** Simultaneously boil yam slices until soft. Drain excess water and mash in a large bowl. Carefully mix fish flakes and mashed yam, a little at a time until you achieve your preferred fish—yam proportions. Add a pinch of salt and mix well. Also add the sliced spring onion. Add oil and mix well using bare hands. Mould mixture into small balls.

**3** Whisk egg, roll balls in egg and place on an oiled baking tray. Bake for about 10 minutes in a pre-heated oven at 190, gas mark 5. Alternatively pan fry for 2-3 minutes on each side.

**4** Serve hot or cold on wreaths of fresh thyme.

# FISH & YAM BALLS

An ideal finger snack. Popularly served at cocktail parties as a starter.

*Preparation Time:* 20 minutes
*Cooking Time:* 40 minutes
*Serves:* 3-4 people

- *2 thick slices of puna or white yam, peel and wash*
- *1 medium size fresh mackerel*
- *Fresh thyme*
- *1 seasoning cube*
- *1 egg*
- *1-2 tablespoons vegetable oil*
- *1 stalk of spring onion or chives, finely slice*

### Cook's note
Mackerel fish works best for this recipe but other oily fish such as salmon can also be used.

Amount of fish/yam you use will depend on your preference for more of one over the other.

Puna yam is the best variety to use for this recipe.

# ROASTED PLANTAIN & PEANUT BUTTER

Popularly called *boli at'epa*, this is the ultimate snack for the common Nigerian. Very basic by nature but nutritious and satisfying enough to have for a lunch time snack.

*Preparation Time:* 2 minutes
*Cooking Time:* 20 minutes
*Serves:* 1 person

- *1 slightly ripe plantain*
- *Crunchy peanut butter*

**Cook's note:** use just ripening plantain for this recipe, with greenish yellow skin.

**1** Carefully remove the plantain skin, rub with a little salt and allow to stand for about 5 minutes. Slice plantain across its length or as preferred.

**2** Heat oven to 190, gas mark 5. Place plantain slices on a baking rack and put in the oven. Bake for 10-15 minutes. Turn plantain slices on their sides at intervals to ensure even roasting.

**3** While still hot, spread peanut butter on plantain slices. Serve immediately.

# GARI GRANULES & GROUNDNUTS

**1** In a large bowl, pour the *gari* granules. Add some fresh drinking water, briskly stir and strain off the fluff which by now is floating in the bowl.

**2** Now add some ice cubes, sugar to taste and pour more drinking water. Allow to settle for a minute and serve with groundnuts.

**3** *Gari* prepared this way may also be eaten with fried fish, *moin-moin*, *akara* or sometimes vegetable stews.

When prepared with iced cold water, *gari* makes a very refreshing snack.

*Preparation Time:* 5 minutes
*Serves:* 1 person

½ *cup of gari granules* •
*2 handfuls of groundnuts* •
*Sugar* •
*Ice* •
*Spring water* •

# FISH PIE

Pies are usually eaten as snacks and often made with meat, but fish pies are also popular. A common lunch time snack.

*Preparation Time:* 10 minutes
*Cooking Time:* 20 minutes
*Serves:* 4 people

*500g Of short crust pastry (flour, butter, water and pinch of salt, alternatively use ready made short crust pastry obtainable from all leading supermarkets)* •
*1 small mackerel fish* •
*1 egg* •
*1 seasoning cube* •
*1 stalk of spring onion* •
*½ cup of fresh milk* •
*1 small onion* •
*fresh thyme* •

Cook's note: mackerel is best for this recipe.

**1** Clean and steam fish for about 5 minutes to enable easy removal of bones. Remove bones, flake fish and place in bowl. Add milk, a teaspoon of thyme, and seasoning cube. Simmer over low heat for 3-5 minutes. Then add chopped spring onion. Add some water to ensure fish mix is moist. Stir and set aside.

**2** Use ready made short crust pastry (or make some using flour, butter, water and a pinch of salt). Carefully roll out pastry on a board. Cut the pastry as desired, core and add the fish mix. Seal pastry edges with a fork. Separate the egg yolk, whisk briefly and use to glaze pie using a soft brush. Pierce holes in the pies to allow steam to escape.

**3** Bake in the oven for about 20 minutes at 190 gas mark 5 or until well browned and cooked inside. Remove from oven and let rest for about 10 minutes. Serve warm or cold.

# ROASTED MAIZE

Maize is a seasonal crop enjoyed throughout Nigeria especially during the raining season. Maize can be boiled or roasted and typically sold on the streets as a snack. Popularly referred to as the 'mouth organ'.

**1** In a bowl add about a litre of water and a teaspoon of salt. Submerge maize in the salted water for about 15 minutes.

**2** Remove maize cobs and shake off excess water. Place on a baking tray and roast in oven for about 15—20 minutes at 190 (gas mark 5) or until evenly browned. Also place the *ube* pears, if using, in the oven and roast for about 5 minutes.

**3** Remove maize from the oven, spread with some butter and serve with *ube* pears.

*Preparation Time:* 2 minutes
*Steeping Time:* 15 minutes
*Cooking Time:* 20 minutes
*Serves:* 1 person

• *2 fresh maize on the cob, peel off husk*
• *Butter (optional)*
• *4 small ube pears (optional)*

Cook's note: use fresh maize, preferably still covered in its leaves for this recipe. You can make some tea by boiling the maize / corn silk.

*Ube* belongs to the same family as avocado pear.

# TIGER PRAWNS WITH SPICY DIP

*Preparation Time:* 10 minutes
*Cooking Time:* 30 minutes
*Serves:* 2 people

- *100ml cooking oil*
- *2 fresh tomatoes*
- *½ red sweet pepper*
- *1 medium onion*
- *12 raw large tiger prawns*
- *1 seasoning cube*
- *1 stalk of spring onion*
- *½ green pepper, finely dice*
- *1 clove of garlic*

**1** Blend tomatoes, garlic, pepper and onion with a cup of water. Heat oil in a sauce pan, add the blend and the seasoning cube. Stir and cook over high heat for 5 minutes. Turn heat down and simmer for 20 minutes. Garnish with diced green peppers.

**2** To cook the prawns, remove veins and rinse clean. Heat a griddle, add a little oil and place prawns. Cook prawns for 1-2 minutes on each side.

**3** Serve on a plate with dip.

In the riverside areas, fish is abundant and fishing is the main source of income for families. A lot of small fish are caught and after the day's fish trade, these small fish are seasoned and deep fried into a delicious snack or light meal. Popular with the Yoruba people in the *isale-eko* area of Lagos, referred to as *yoyo*. This recipe is inspired by *yoyo* as made in *isale-eko*.

# TWO MINUTES NOODLES

**1** Boil water in a small pot. Remove noodles from packet and place in boiling water.

**2** Add the mixed vegetables and noodle seasonings. Also add the cooked chicken breasts and prawns. Stir well and allow water to evaporate. Add oil and flaked dried chilli (if using), stir fry for a few seconds, remove from heat.

**3** Serve hot.

Noodles are now very popular in Nigeria especially among kids. Introduced by Asian migrants, different flavours are available and even more recently *jollof* noodles have been developed!

*Preparation Time:* 5 minutes
*Cooking Time:* 2 minutes
*Serves:* 2 people

*2 packets of your preferred two minute noodles •*
*6 cooked king prawns •*
*Handful of diced cooked chicken breast •*
*Handful of mixed frozen vegetables •*
*2 cups of water •*
*20ml cooking oil •*
*Flaked dried chilli (optional) •*

Vegetarian option: Cook noodles without meat and prawns.

# MOIN-MOIN

*Preparation Time:* 50 minutes
*Cooking Time:* 30 minutes
*Serves:* 4 people

*Moin moin* is a delicious savory pudding which can be eaten as a breakfast meal with *ogi* or as a light meal eaten with rice, bread, *eko* or *asaro*.

2 cups of African brown beans ('oloyin') •
4 hard boiled eggs (optional) •
½ cup of fresh milk (optional) •
2 tablespoons of tomato paste •
1 large onion •
5 seasoning cubes •
100ml cooking oil •
4 soufflé cups (or broad banana leaves or foil paper) •
1 scotch bonnet yellow, remove seeds (optional) •
1 medium red sweet pepper •

**1** Soak beans in water for about 30 minutes. Peel skin off beans by rubbing together to reveal the white bean shells. Discard the skin and rinse well. Blend beans, pepper, tomato paste and onion with 2 cups of water into a paste. Slowly add more water a little at a time to aid blending.

**2** Transfer blend into a mixing bowl and mix continuously for about 2-3 minutes. Add ½ cup of warm water and ½ cup of milk. Continue to mix until you get a moderately runny consistency. Dissolve the seasoning cubes in 3 tablespoons of hot water and add to the paste. Add oil and continue to mix for another 2 minutes. (You may use a hand held mixer).

**3** Scoop blend into soufflé cups and add one whole boiled egg per cup. If using foil or leaves, make pouches from the leaves or foil and scoop portions of the paste into them, then seal to ensure paste does not leak. Steam for about 30 minutes.

**4** Eat on its own or with rice dishes, 'eko' or soaked 'gari' granules. Can be served hot or cold.

### Cook's note
Soaking the beans softens them and makes them easier to blend. Ensure that beans are blended into a fine smooth paste. This can be achieved from a continuous blast of the blender. Improve the overall consistency by mixing blend with hot water. Prolonged mixing improves texture.

Bean flour may be used in place of whole brown beans. Make a paste by adding warn water to the bean flour and continue preparation from step 2 .

A variety of ingredients can be included in the *moin-moin*. Small pieces of cooked ox liver, boiled fish pieces particularly mackerel or corn beef may be added. Sliced boiled eggs are most commonly added.

*Olo* variety of brown beans is best for *moin-moin* even though the *Oloyin* variety may also be used.

Snacks, Desserts & Drinks

# AFRICAN SNAILS SAUTÉ

*Preparation Time:* 10 minutes
*Cooking Time:* 20 minutes
*Serves:* 4 people

Snails are a delicacy enjoyed throughout Nigeria. Typically cooked and served in stews or soups, snails are also fried and eaten as a snack or starter.
*Native name(s): igbin*

4 giant African snails, shelled and cleaned •
1 medium onion, dice •
1 scotch bonnet, remove seeds and finely chop
(optional) •
2 small tomatoes, dice •
¼ small green sweet pepper, dice •
½ small red sweet pepper, dice •
3 stalks of spring onions, slice •
1 teaspoon freshly chopped thyme •
1 small lemon •
1 seasoning cube •
100ml vegetable or blended olive oil •

**1** Wash snails in running water. Cut lemon and rub on snails to remove excess slime. Cut snails into equal halves and trim off unwanted internal parts.

**2** Place snails in a small pan, add some water, a pinch of salt and steam for about 5 minutes. Drain and set aside.

**3** Heat oil in another pan, add onion, thyme, tomatoes, green & red pepper and scotch bonnet (if using). Stir. Then add the seasoning cube. Also add a sprinkling of water and leave to simmer for 5 minutes. Add the snails, stir. Finally add the spring onions and simmer for a further 2 minutes.

**4** Serve with a cold drink.

**Cook's note**
Snails must be cooked quickly to avoid them becoming rubbery. They can also be cooked in stews or soups.

Snails are mollusks and rich in protein. Research also shows that snails are rich in minerals such as potassium, phosphorous and magnesium. They are low in fat and believed to help in lowering cholesterol.

Snacks, Desserts & Drinks

# OGI & AKARA

*Preparation Time:* 50 minutes
*Cooking Time:* 20 minutes
*Serves:* 4 people

An ideal and nutritionally complete breakfast meal. *Ogi* is a product of ground and fermented maize or corn, millet or sorghum.
*Native name(s): kose de kosai, akamu, koko*

4 portions of ogi paste or 200g of ogi powder •
2 cups of African brown beans ('olo' variety),
pick chaff and stones •
1 stalk of spring onion, finely slice •
2 small tomatoes •
2 seasoning cubes •
2 medium onions •
4 prawns, chop •
Salt and sugar •
Evaporated milk •
Palm oil or vegetable oil for frying •

**1** Soak beans in water for about 30 minutes. Peel skin off by rubbing together to reveal the white bean shells. Separate these from the skin and rinse well. Blend beans, tomato paste and onion with some warm water (1-2 cups) into a paste. Slowly add water a little at a time to aid blending. Transfer paste into a mixing bowl and mix well for about 3 minutes, you may use a handheld mixer. Add some water and keep mixing until you get a smooth and moderately runny consistency. Dissolve the seasoning cubes in 2 tablespoons of hot water and add to the paste. Add the spring onions and chopped prawns. Mix well. (Similar recipe on page 80)

**2** Deep fry the mixture in dollops, for about 5 minutes depending on size, or until it turns golden brown. Drain and set aside and keep warm.

**3** Simultaneously place the *ogi* paste/powder into a pot, mix with 350ml of cold water and stir well into a runny mix, avoid lumps forming. Then add 200ml of boiling water into the *ogi* mix, stirring continuously. Now place pot on moderate heat and boil for a further 2-3 minutes, stirring continuously as it thickens. This step can be carried out simultaneously with step 2.

**4** Transfer *ogi* into a bowl, add evaporated milk, and sugar as desired. Serve with the fried *akara*.

### Cook's note
Some *ogi* paste or powder have a sharp and sour taste which is developed during the fermentation process. The sharp/tangy taste is desirable by some.

# MUSHY BEANS

*Preparation Time:* 10 minutes
*Cooking Time:* 50 minutes
*Serves:* 4 people

This dish was introduced to Nigerians by immigrants from Benin and Togo republics. Very popular dish eaten as breakfast or light evening meal. Best eaten with boiled yams or hard dough bread.

*Native name(s):  ewa aganyin*

3 cups African brown beans ('oloyin' variety),
remove chaff and stones •
Salt and sugar •
4 small tomatoes, finely slice •
1½ litre of water •
2 small onions finely slice •
100ml of palm oil •
100ml of vegetable oil •
2 seasoning cubes •
1 tablespoon of ground crayfish •
Hard dough bread •

**1** Wash beans and place in a pressure cooker. Add water, 1 seasoning cube, cover and cook beans under pressure until very soft—say 20 minutes (depending on the quantity of beans). Remove cooker from heat or turn off the pressure cooking. Carefully open and stir.

**2** Now continue to cook under low heat, adding 500ml of hot water and vegetable oil, stir well and mash up beans. Add salt and sugar to taste. Cook under low heat for another 10-15 minutes. Continue to stir to achieve a soft mash with a smooth consistency.

**3** Heat the palm oil in a separate sauce pan until it starts to smoke, add onion and tomatoes, this may cause the sauce to flambé. Stir carefully. Add some salt and 1 seasoning cube. Under low heat, continue to fry until onions caramelize. Sprinkle the ground crayfish. Stir.

**4** Serve mashed beans with sauce and toasted, buttered hard dough bread.

Beans fulfil many dietary requirements, including provision of folates, potassium, and are very high in protein, fibre and low in fat.

# TROPICAL FRUITS SALAD

1 In a large bowl, add the fruit chunks and mix carefully with a wooden spoon. Add the pineapple juice last. Stir gently, cover bowl with cling film and chill for about one hour in a refrigerator.

2 Scoop fruit mix into dessert bowls with some of the residual juice and serve.

Fruits generally are a good source of vitamins and minerals. Pineapples are rich in manganese, vitamin C, B1 & B6, copper, dietary fibre. Papaya is considered to be one of the healthiest fruits to eat!

There are different varieties of tropical and exotic fruits in Nigeria. They are normally eaten in their raw state, usually after a meal or as a lunch or evening time refreshment.

*Preparation Time:* 10 minutes
*Serves:* 4 people

- *1 mango, wash peel and cut into small chunks*
- *1 small papaya, wash, peel skin, remove seeds and cut into small chunks*
- *1 medium guava, wash and cut into small chunks*
- *I tangerine or tangelo, peel, part into segments, remove seeds and dice*
- *2 cups of pineapple juice*

Most fruits can be used in this recipe but to get the best results, use only well ripen ones. Ensure you are able to achieve a balance of sweet and sour tastes from the fruits you choose.

100

# BUSH TEA WITH CAKES

Bush tea is the African equivalent to herbal teas, made from a variety of barks, herbs and leaves. Largely drunk for its medicinal properties and often referred to as *agbo*. The tea in this recipe is believed to act as a blood tonic.

*Preparation Time:* 15 minutes
*Cooking Time:* 35 minutes
*Serves:* 2 people

### Tea Ingredients
- 3 stalks of millet •
- Evaporated milk •
- Sugar •

### Cake ingredients
- 300g self raising flour •
- 200g sugar •
- 3 eggs •
- 150g of butter •
- Essence of millet tea •

**1** To make the essence, wash and boil a stalk of millet in 500ml of water until an intense pink liquid is achieved. Slowly boil to reduce the liquid into essence (to about 50ml). Cool.

**2** Sieve flour and make a fluffy batter with the eggs, butter and sugar. In same circular movement, add the essence of the millet tea from step 1 and mix well. Transfer batter into a baking tin and bake in a preheated oven at 185 gas mark 4 for about 20 minutes or until baked. Cool and slice.

**3** Wash and boil remaining millet stalks in 1 litre of hot water. Allow to infuse for 2 minutes, pour into a teacup, add sugar and milk. Serve with a slice of cake.

# TROPICAL FRUITS SMOOTHIE

Nigerian fruits are seasonal and there are very little known methods of preserving them. Increasingly, new ideas are emerging on how these fruits may be preserved for longer and their use maximized. One of such new ideas is to create smoothies.

*Preparation Time:* 10 minutes
*Serves:* 4 people

- *1 mango, wash, peel skin & cut into small pieces*
- *1 guava, wash and cut into small pieces*
- *3-4 cups pineapple juice.*
- *½ very ripe papaya, peel and cut into small pieces*
- *1 slice of red sweet peppers chop finely (optional)*

To get the best results, use well ripen fruits when their sugar levels are at the highest.

**1** Transfer fruit pieces and pineapple juice into a smoothie maker or a blender and blend. Stir in the chopped sweet pepper. Chill immediately.

**2** Serve chilled.

# TROPICAL FRUIT PUNCH

- ¼ cup of ogogoro or gin (optional)
- Crushed ice
- 200ml sorrel concentrate
- 1 cup of pineapple juice
- 2-3 cups of spring water
- 5 petals of dried roselle flower (rinse)

*Preparation Time:* 5 minutes
*Serves:* makes 1 litre

This punch is locally called *sobo*. Its main ingredient, roselle is rich in vitamin C & antioxidants.

**1** In a large mixing bowl add the sorrel concentrate, pineapple juice and stir well. Add water and mix. Taste for sweetness. Add sugar or water as desired to balance sweetness. Add the roselle petals and *ogogoro* if using. Refrigerate and allow to infuse.

**2** Serve in cocktail glasses with crushed ice and orange slices.

Dried roselle petals steeped in hot water may be used instead of concentrate. A sour tasting brew is produced which can be enhanced by blending with sugarcane juice or sugar, & spices (e.g. cinnamon).

# Acknowledgement

## To God be the Glory.

I feel accomplished with the publishing of this book. As a young adult, I had a list of goals that I dreamt of attaining. I also had a strong desire to make a contribution towards promoting the character, culture and image of my origins, Nigeria.

The 'Contemporary Nigerian Cuisine' cookbook represents the fulfilment of one of my long held goals and the beginning of my contributions towards the up building of the image of my mother land, Nigeria.

I could not have written this book without the support of my husband and children who endured endless requests to taste and comment on the different outcomes from each of the recipes.

My seven year old daughter, Molola, has also began her cooking lessons as she is always there to provide assistance in preparing and presenting the dishes. So has my son Mayowa, who I also discovered has real skills in photography!

Many thanks to Gavin Bond (TNG Food Photography Ltd.) who took the shots of the dishes. Gavin found this project particularly challenging as he had no experience in shooting Nigerian food. I commend his flexibility, patience and creativity which helped to produce the amazing pictures of the dishes. He comes highly recommended.

I would also like to acknowledge the support and assistance of my family; my parents for their prayers and admonitions, my sisters & brothers, my friends especially Bidemi Johnson, and colleagues; for their immense contributions, suggestions, ideas and inspiration.

Special thanks to the readers of this cookbook and all the adventurous cooks out there who have decided to embark on this culinary journey.

God bless.

## GMTV Christmas Kitchen

Funke, took part in the GMTV Christmas Kitchen (United Kingdom Television Network) programme in the run-up to Christmas 2008, preparing the perfect Nigerian Christmas Dinner. She featured the traditional *jollof* rice (see pages 74-75), served with turkey strips roasted with *suya* spices (see pages 20-21) and diced fried plantains (see page 30) with mixed sweet peppers, pictured on page 105.

The programme was shown as part of providing ideas for preparing Christmas Dinners (December 2008).

## A word from the Author

This cookbook is authored for food enthusiasts keen to discover. It is assumed that those trying out the recipes contained in this book have some cooking experience. However, help is at hand for those who may experience difficulties. Register on my website and receive regular updates, food ideas and find out what is new or happening on the Nigerian food scene. Please visit,

### www.contemporarynigeriancuisine.com

*Many thanks*
*Funke*

# About the Author

Funke Koleosho is an avid lover of Nigerian food after having learned the techniques of traditional Nigerian cooking from a very young age.

She moved to the United Kingdom where her methods of cooking and presenting Nigerian dishes have been influenced by her new environment.

Funke is passionate about African cooking and believes that Nigerian foods compare favourably with foods from around the world in their wholesomeness and nutritional value.

She loves to entertain and thrill guests with her creative methods of cooking and food presentation. She is known as the perfect hostess among her circle of friends and relatives.

Funke has a bachelors degree in Food Science, lives in a suburb of London with her husband and two children. She pursues a professional career in the city of London.

First edition

On GMTV set

*Jollof* rice and turkey strips as featured on GMTV

# INDEX

# Shopping for ingredients

Below are the names and descriptions of some ingredients used in Nigerian cooking and how to shop for them.

### African Giant Snail
A delicacy desired for its soft and succulent texture. Can be purchased live still in its shell or cleaned and frozen.

### Brown beans
Similar to black eye peas but brown in colour. Sold in bags in 2 varieties; olo and oloyin

### Catfish
Sold fresh or frozen. Two species black (aro) and gray (obokun).

### Dried fish
Sold whole or in broken pieces in small packets.

### Efo
Multipurpose Yoruba name for green leafy vegetables. Sold as fresh produce. Some blanched frozen brands are also available.

### Egusi, agushi
Melon and pumpkin seeds sold whole or ground and packed in bags.

### Fufu, akpu
Starchy dough made from fermented cassava. Fufu may be purchased as a ready meal or cassava flour which is further processed before use. Available in different brands.

### Garden eggs
Small green/white, glossy skinned African equivalent of aubergines or eggplants. Sold as fresh produce.

### Gari
Starchy granules made from fermented cassava. Sold in bags in different brands and varieties, white & yellow.

### Groundnuts
African name for peanuts. Shelled and sold in bottles. Also available as groundnut paste; substitute with peanut butter.

### Guava
A creamy fruit with some similarities to fig. Has tiny seeds embedded in its inner fleshy parts. Sold as a fresh produce.

### Locust beans iru, dadawa
Pungent but desirable condiment used in soups and stews. Sold as fresh or frozen. Processed into dadawa cubes, by Cadbury Nigeria . Also available as ground dadawa.

### Mango
Sweet fruit with creamy and fibrous flesh. Sold as a fresh produce.

### Obe, ofe, miya, stew ingredients
Versatile sauce made from tomatoes, sweet peppers, onions and chillies. Some bottled sauces are available online. Basic ingredients are fresh tomatoes, chillis, red peppers and onions. Bottled obe sauce is available for sale online.

### Okra, Gumbo
Okra fingers are gelatinous pods used as an agent to thicken soups. Sold as fresh or frozen produce.

### Ogbonna, apon
Derived from dried bush mango seeds, used to thicken soups. Sold as whole seeds or ground/powdered.

### Ogogoro, local gin
Local alcoholic drink distilled from palm wine. Sold in bottles.

### Ogi, akamo, koko
Fermented ground maize. Sold as powder or as a paste. Ogi is usually made into a breakfast porridge. It can also be processed to make eko and eaten with a variety of vegetables and soups.

### Palm oil
Bright red oil derived from palm kernels. Different brands available, sold in bottles or kegs.

### Pammy, palm wine
Naturally fermented juice from the palm tree, drunk as a beverage. Freshly tapped palm wine has little alcohol content, but this increases with age due to fermentation. Sold in bottles.

### Plantain
A starchy fruit vegetable of the banana family. Can be cooked in its 3 different stages of ripeness. Found in most open markets as a fresh produce.

### Roselle, ishapa pupa
Dried flowers of roselle plant used to make a fruit punch called sobo. Roselle can be purchased fresh or dried in packets or as a bottled cordial. Also called sorrel by the West Indians .

### Scotch bonnet
Red or yellow hot chilli. Used a lot in Nigerian cooking. Sold as fresh produce.

### Stockfish, okporoko
Freeze dried cod fish used in vegetable stews and soups. Sold whole or in small pieces.

### Tilapia
Freshwater fish rich in omega oils and recognised as the safest fish to consume due to its very low residual mercury content. Sold fresh or frozen.

### Tuwo
Rice dish made by boiling and mashing rice into a paste. Sticky rice is preferred to make tuwo but any long grain or basmati rice can be used.

### Ugwu, pumpkin leaves
Seasonal, leafy vegetable. Sold fresh in bunches or dried.

### Yam
A starchy root vegetable. There are different varieties such as puna, Ghana or white, water yam to name a few. Sold as fresh produce. Pounded yam powder is sold in bags in various brands.